"God, in his wisdom, gave us sure guidance on how to pray—it's called the Psalms. He also gave us words of wisdom about prayer stretched across the span of the whole Bible. In *Teach Us to Pray* Tim Beals leads us back to the Bible's wisdom about prayer. I shall keep this book close at hand—it's destined to become a book that will help many learn to pray all over again—this time by listening to divine wisdom about prayer."

> —SCOT MCKNIGHT, Karl A. Olsson Professor in
> Religious Studies, North Park University;
> author, *The Jesus Creed*

"The key to a growing relationship with the God of all creation is a living communication with him through the personal dialogue of listening and speaking. *Teach Us to Pray* is a welcome resource that arranges many of the wonderful prayers of the Bible into a clear and accessible format that will equip the reader to have a more rich and meaningful life of communion with the Lord."

> —KEN BOA, President, Reflection Ministries;
> author, *Conformed to His Image*

"Praying the Word is a powerful and time-tested path to becoming effective in prayer. Tim Beals's compilation of Scripture as a tool for praying is thoughtful and well laid out. Reading *Teach Us to Pray* was an unexpected delight, and I look forward to using it often as a resource in my prayer library."

> —TED KALLMAN, Director, "Wrestling Team"
> Prayer Ministry, Mars Hill Bible Church,
> Grandville, MI; coauthor of *Stark Raving
> Obedience*

S0-AQH-797

TEACH US TO PRAY

TEACH *Us to* PRAY

365 PRAYERS *from the Bible*

TIMOTHY J. BEALS

EDITOR

CROSSWAY BOOKS
WHEATON, ILLINOIS

Teach Us to Pray

Copyright © 2008 by Timothy J. Beals

Published by Crossway Books
a publishing ministry of Good News Publishers
1300 Crescent Street
Wheaton, Illinois 60187

Published in association with Credo Communications LLC, Grand Rapids, MI 49525; www.credocommunications.net.

Cover design: J. McGrath

Cover photo: Getty Images

First printing 2008

Printed in the United States of America

PDF ISBN: 978-1-4335-0480-8

Mobipocket ISBN: 978-1-4335-0481-5

Library of Congress Cataloging-in-Publication Data
Teach us to pray : 365 prayers from the Bible / Timothy J. Beals, editor.
    p. cm.
  Includes bibliographical references.
  ISBN 978-1-58134-967-2 (tpb)
  1. Bible—Prayers. 2. Prayer—Christianity. I. Beals, Tim. II. Bible. English. English Standard. Selections. 2008.
BS680.P64T425   2008
242'.722—dc22   2008007549

VP		17	16	15	14	13	12	11	10	09	08
14	13	12	11	10	9	8	7	6	5	4	3	2	1

To
Dad and Mom,

who taught me how to pray

and to

Cheri, Marie, and Carmen,

who show me how to pray

Contents

The Language of Prayer

We learn to pray in the same way we learn to speak a language: first by copying and then by making what we copy our own. This all-in-one volume defines the language of prayer, serving both as a primer and as a reader for those who long to begin or to enrich their prayer experience, with essential selections from the Bible as their foundation.

For millennia, both Israel and the church have regarded the Psalms as the prayer book of the people of God, the foundation of all prayer. Even the Lord's Prayer is a distillation of all the grand themes of the Psalter. The purpose of this collection is to encourage the reader to learn how to pray the Psalms and the rest of Scripture by providing:

- the language for prayer, making this little volume a prayer book for today that makes explicit the relationship between prayer and the timeless Scriptures (in Part 1)
- a pattern of the rich varieties of prayer and the diverse occasions upon which we might feel drawn to pray the Scriptures (in Part 2)

• an exploration of the Jesus Prayer, which our Lord taught his disciples when they asked, "Lord, teach us to pray . . ." (in the Afterword)

This is not a book designed to explore the age-old questions of why we pray, how we pray, and when we pray—all topics that have been fruitfully discussed, if not settled, in other texts. We assume here that believers want to pray—indeed, *have* to pray—but are frequently bewildered by what to pray, having become disillusioned by their own ineffective, self-generated attempts at meaningful prayer.

In the course of reading the Psalms and other Scripture-based prayers in *Teach Us to Pray*, we hope that you will come to:

• understand better the priority of prayer throughout the Scriptures
• develop the habit of praying Scripture and cultivating a heart for the Savior and his priorities for your life today
• discover the power of praying God's Word back to him

Throughout their accounts of Jesus' life and ministry, the Gospel writers attest to the priority he placed on prayer (Luke 5:16) and to the many uses he made of Scripture in his own prayers. We don't know what Jesus prayed in his many private sessions alone with God. But we get a hint of his focus and priorities when we concentrate on his public, recorded prayers. In the longest of these, sometimes called the High-Priestly Prayer (John 17:1–26), Jesus echoes lines from nearly one-fourth of the books that constitute the Hebrew Bible (Exodus, Leviticus, 2 Samuel, 1 Kings, Psalms, Jeremiah, and Daniel).

And when he was facing extraordinary distress—in the Garden of Gethsemane and on the cross—we overhear our Lord borrowing directly from Scripture, usually from the Psalms. In Gethsemane (Matthew 26:36–45) Jesus prayed three times, "saying the same words" in each instance (v. 44), vocabulary borrowed from Psalm 40 and Isaiah 50. And again as he hung dying on the cross, Jesus expressed his prayers in the language of Scripture. "My God, my God, why have you forsaken me?" (Matthew 27:46) is borrowed from Psalm 22:1, and "Father, into your hands I commit my spirit" (Luke 23:46) is a direct quotation from Psalm 31:5.

Charles Spurgeon calls to our attention that when Jesus most needed to pray, this grand, original thinker saw no need to be innovative or extemporaneous:

> How instructive is this great truth that the Incarnate Word lived on the Inspired Word! It was food to him, as it is to us; and . . . if Christ thus lived upon the Word of God, should not you and I do the same? . . . I think it well worthy of your constant remembrance that, even in death, our blessed Master showed the ruling passion of his spirit, so that his last words were a quotation from Scripture.[1]

To pray through, in, and from Scripture is to pray according to God's will. The Bible supplies the language— the vocabulary and grammar—of prayer. Learning to pray the Psalms (and all Scripture) provides us with the right words and helps us make those words our own. It puts the focus where it belongs—on God, not on ourselves and our perceived needs and feelings. Our own self-generated prayers quickly become monotonous. It's not that God is boring, but that we are, in terms of the spiritual ruts and tedious clichés that have too often come to characterize our prayers. Biblical prayer raises up our desires to heaven, where both they and we can be transformed and our pleasure in prayer renewed.

PART ONE

Psalms

BOOK ONE

PSALM 1

A study in contrasts: the godly way and the wicked way.

Blessed is the man
   who walks not in the counsel of the wicked,
nor stands in the way of sinners,
   nor sits in the seat of scoffers;
but his delight is in the law of the LORD,
   and on his law he meditates day and night.

He is like a tree
   planted by streams of water
that yields its fruit in its season,
   and its leaf does not wither.
In all that he does, he prospers.
The wicked are not so,
   but are like chaff that the wind drives away.

Therefore the wicked will not stand in the judgment,
   nor sinners in the congregation of the righteous;
for the LORD knows the way of the righteous,
   but the way of the wicked will perish.

PSALM 2

God will protect the One he has anointed.

Why do the nations rage
   and the peoples plot in vain?

Psalms

The kings of the earth set themselves,
    and the rulers take counsel together,
    against the LORD and against his Anointed, saying,
"Let us burst their bonds apart
    and cast away their cords from us."

He who sits in the heavens laughs;
    the Lord holds them in derision.
Then he will speak to them in his wrath,
    and terrify them in his fury, saying,
"As for me, I have set my King
    on Zion, my holy hill."

I will tell of the decree:
The LORD said to me, "You are my Son;
    today I have begotten you.
Ask of me, and I will make the nations your heritage,
    and the ends of the earth your possession.
You shall break them with a rod of iron
    and dash them in pieces like a potter's vessel."

Now therefore, O kings, be wise;
    be warned, O rulers of the earth.
Serve the LORD with fear,
    and rejoice with trembling.
Kiss the Son,
    lest he be angry, and you perish in the way,
    for his wrath is quickly kindled.
Blessed are all who take refuge in him.

PSALM 5

The Lord hates evil but is a refuge to the righteous.

Give ear to my words, O LORD;
        consider my groaning.
Give attention to the sound of my cry,
        my King and my God,
        for to you do I pray.
O LORD, in the morning you hear my voice;
        in the morning I prepare a sacrifice for you and watch.

For you are not a God who delights in wickedness;
        evil may not dwell with you.
The boastful shall not stand before your eyes;
        you hate all evildoers.
You destroy those who speak lies;
        the LORD abhors the bloodthirsty and deceitful man.

But I, through the abundance of your steadfast love,
        will enter your house.
I will bow down toward your holy temple
        in the fear of you.
Lead me, O LORD, in your righteousness
        because of my enemies;
        make your way straight before me.

For there is no truth in their mouth;
        their inmost self is destruction;
their throat is an open grave;
        they flatter with their tongue.
Make them bear their guilt, O God;

let them fall by their own counsels;
because of the abundance of their transgressions cast them out,
for they have rebelled against you.

But let all who take refuge in you rejoice;
let them ever sing for joy,
and spread your protection over them,
that those who love your name may exult in you.
For you bless the righteous, O LORD;
you cover him with favor as with a shield.

PSALM 8

People have an important place in the majesty of all creation.

O LORD, our Lord,
how majestic is your name in all the earth!
You have set your glory above the heavens.
Out of the mouth of babies and infants,
you have established strength because of your foes,
to still the enemy and the avenger.

When I look at your heavens, the work of your fingers,
the moon and the stars, which you have set in place,
what is man that you are mindful of him,
and the son of man that you care for him?

Yet you have made him a little lower than the heavenly beings
and crowned him with glory and honor.
You have given him dominion over the works of your hands;
you have put all things under his feet,
all sheep and oxen,

and also the beasts of the field,
the birds of the heavens, and the fish of the sea,
whatever passes along the paths of the seas.

O LORD, our Lord,
how majestic is your name in all the earth!

PSALM 12

In the midst of a faithless world, God remains faithful.

Save, O LORD, for the godly one is gone;
for the faithful have vanished from among the children of man.
Everyone utters lies to his neighbor;
with flattering lips and a double heart they speak.

May the LORD cut off all flattering lips,
the tongue that makes great boasts,
those who say, "With our tongue we will prevail,
our lips are with us; who is master over us?"

"Because the poor are plundered, because the needy groan,
I will now arise," says the LORD;
"I will place him in the safety for which he longs."
The words of the LORD are pure words,
like silver refined in a furnace on the ground,
purified seven times.

You, O LORD, will keep them;
you will guard us from this generation forever.
On every side the wicked prowl,
as vileness is exalted among the children of man.

PSALM 13

As agonizing as it can be to wait upon the Lord, there is assurance in his salvation.

How long, O LORD? Will you forget me forever?
    How long will you hide your face from me?
How long must I take counsel in my soul
    and have sorrow in my heart all the day?
How long shall my enemy be exalted over me?

Consider and answer me, O LORD my God;
    light up my eyes, lest I sleep the sleep of death,
lest my enemy say, "I have prevailed over him,"
    lest my foes rejoice because I am shaken.

But I have trusted in your steadfast love;
    my heart shall rejoice in your salvation.
I will sing to the LORD,
    because he has dealt bountifully with me.

PSALM 14

The world has turned its back on God.

The fool says in his heart, "There is no God."
    They are corrupt, they do abominable deeds,
    there is none who does good.

The LORD looks down from heaven on the children of man,
    to see if there are any who understand,
    who seek after God.

They have all turned aside; together they have become corrupt;

there is none who does good,
not even one.

Have they no knowledge, all the evildoers
    who eat up my people as they eat bread
    and do not call upon the LORD?

There they are in great terror,
    for God is with the generation of the righteous.
You would shame the plans of the poor,
    but the LORD *is his refuge.*

Oh, that salvation for Israel would come out of Zion!
    When the LORD *restores the fortunes of his people,*
    let Jacob rejoice, let Israel be glad.

PSALM 15

A lesson in righteousness: practices pleasing to the Lord.

O LORD, who shall sojourn in your tent?
    Who shall dwell on your holy hill?

He who walks blamelessly and does what is right
    and speaks truth in his heart;
who does not slander with his tongue
    and does no evil to his neighbor,
    nor takes up a reproach against his friend;
in whose eyes a vile person is despised,
    but who honors those who fear the LORD;
who swears to his own hurt and does not change;

who does not put out his money at interest
    and does not take a bribe against the innocent.
He who does these things shall never be moved.

Psalm 16

God will not abandon the one who seeks him.

Preserve me, O God, for in you I take refuge.
I say to the LORD, "You are my Lord;
    I have no good apart from you."

As for the saints in the land, they are the excellent ones,
    in whom is all my delight.

The sorrows of those who run after another god shall multiply;
    their drink offerings of blood I will not pour out
    or take their names on my lips.

The LORD is my chosen portion and my cup;
    you hold my lot.
The lines have fallen for me in pleasant places;
    indeed, I have a beautiful inheritance.

I bless the LORD who gives me counsel;
    in the night also my heart instructs me.
I have set the LORD always before me;
    because he is at my right hand, I shall not be shaken.

Therefore my heart is glad, and my whole being rejoices;
    my flesh also dwells secure.
For you will not abandon my soul to Sheol,
    or let your holy one see corruption.

You make known to me the path of life;
>in your presence there is fullness of joy;
>at your right hand are pleasures forevermore.

PSALM 17

God will hear the cry of the righteous and will protect them.

Hear a just cause, O LORD; attend to my cry!
>Give ear to my prayer from lips free of deceit!
From your presence let my vindication come!
>Let your eyes behold the right!

You have tried my heart, you have visited me by night,
>you have tested me, and you will find nothing;
>I have purposed that my mouth will not transgress.
With regard to the works of man, by the word of your lips
>I have avoided the ways of the violent.
My steps have held fast to your paths;
>my feet have not slipped.

I call upon you, for you will answer me, O God;
>incline your ear to me; hear my words.
Wondrously show your steadfast love,
>O Savior of those who seek refuge
>from their adversaries at your right hand.

Keep me as the apple of your eye;
>hide me in the shadow of your wings,
from the wicked who do me violence,
>my deadly enemies who surround me.

They close their hearts to pity;
with their mouths they speak arrogantly.
They have now surrounded our steps;
they set their eyes to cast us to the ground.
He is like a lion eager to tear,
as a young lion lurking in ambush.

Arise, O LORD! Confront him, subdue him!
Deliver my soul from the wicked by your sword,
from men by your hand, O LORD,
from men of the world whose portion is in this life.
You fill their womb with treasure;
they are satisfied with children,
and they leave their abundance to their infants.

As for me, I shall behold your face in righteousness;
when I awake, I shall be satisfied with your likeness.

PSALM 19

Great is the glory of God, as reflected in his creation and in his wonderful law.

The heavens declare the glory of God,
and the sky above proclaims his handiwork.
Day to day pours out speech,
and night to night reveals knowledge.
There is no speech, nor are there words,
whose voice is not heard.
Their measuring line goes out through all the earth,
and their words to the end of the world.
In them he has set a tent for the sun,
which comes out like a bridegroom leaving his chamber,

and, like a strong man, runs its course with joy.
Its rising is from the end of the heavens,
and its circuit to the end of them,
and there is nothing hidden from its heat.

The law of the LORD is perfect,
reviving the soul;
the testimony of the LORD is sure,
making wise the simple;
the precepts of the LORD are right,
rejoicing the heart;
the commandment of the LORD is pure,
enlightening the eyes;
the fear of the LORD is clean,
enduring forever;
the rules of the LORD are true,
and righteous altogether.
More to be desired are they than gold,
even much fine gold;
sweeter also than honey
and drippings of the honeycomb.
Moreover, by them is your servant warned;
in keeping them there is great reward.

Who can discern his errors?
Declare me innocent from hidden faults.
Keep back your servant also from presumptuous sins;
let them not have dominion over me!
Then I shall be blameless,
and innocent of great transgression.

Let the words of my mouth and the meditation of my heart
    be acceptable in your sight,
        O Lord, my rock and my redeemer.

Psalm 22

A plea that God might both be present now and be praised by future generations.

My God, my God, why have you forsaken me?
    Why are you so far from saving me, from the words of my
        groaning?
O my God, I cry by day, but you do not answer,
    and by night, but I find no rest.

Yet you are holy,
    enthroned on the praises of Israel.
In you our fathers trusted;
    they trusted, and you delivered them.
To you they cried and were rescued;
    in you they trusted and were not put to shame.

But I am a worm and not a man,
    scorned by mankind and despised by the people.
All who see me mock me;
    they make mouths at me; they wag their heads;
"He trusts in the Lord; let him deliver him;
    let him rescue him, for he delights in him!"

Yet you are he who took me from the womb;
    you made me trust you at my mother's breasts.
On you was I cast from my birth,
    and from my mother's womb you have been my God.

Be not far from me,
> *for trouble is near,*
> *and there is none to help.*

Many bulls encompass me;
> *strong bulls of Bashan surround me;*
they open wide their mouths at me,
> *like a ravening and roaring lion.*

I am poured out like water,
> *and all my bones are out of joint;*
my heart is like wax;
> *it is melted within my breast;*
my strength is dried up like a potsherd,
> *and my tongue sticks to my jaws;*
> *you lay me in the dust of death.*

For dogs encompass me;
> *a company of evildoers encircles me;*
they have pierced my hands and feet—
I can count all my bones—
they stare and gloat over me;
they divide my garments among them,
> *and for my clothing they cast lots.*

But you, O LORD, do not be far off!
> *O you my help, come quickly to my aid!*
Deliver my soul from the sword,
> *my precious life from the power of the dog!*
> *Save me from the mouth of the lion!*
You have rescued me from the horns of the wild oxen!

I will tell of your name to my brothers;

    in the midst of the congregation I will praise you:

You who fear the Lord*, praise him!*

    All you offspring of Jacob, glorify him,

    and stand in awe of him, all you offspring of Israel!

For he has not despised or abhorred

    the affliction of the afflicted,

and he has not hidden his face from him,

    but has heard, when he cried to him.

From you comes my praise in the great congregation;

    my vows I will perform before those who fear him.

The afflicted shall eat and be satisfied;

    those who seek him shall praise the Lord*!*

    May your hearts live forever!

All the ends of the earth shall remember

    and turn to the Lord*,*

and all the families of the nations

    shall worship before you.

For kingship belongs to the Lord*,*

    and he rules over the nations.

All the prosperous of the earth eat and worship;

    before him shall bow all who go down to the dust,

    even the one who could not keep himself alive.

Posterity shall serve him;

    it shall be told of the Lord to the coming generation;

they shall come and proclaim his righteousness to a people yet

        unborn,

    that he has done it.

PSALM 23
The Great Shepherd protects and provides for his sheep.

The LORD is my shepherd; I shall not want.
He makes me lie down in green pastures.
He leads me beside still waters.
He restores my soul.
He leads me in paths of righteousness
for his name's sake.

Even though I walk through the valley of the shadow of death,
I will fear no evil,
for you are with me;
your rod and your staff,
they comfort me.

You prepare a table before me
in the presence of my enemies;
you anoint my head with oil;
my cup overflows.
Surely goodness and mercy shall follow me
all the days of my life,
and I shall dwell in the house of the LORD forever.

PSALM 24
God is the King of Glory.

The earth is the LORD's and the fullness thereof,
the world and those who dwell therein,
for he has founded it upon the seas
and established it upon the rivers.

Who shall ascend the hill of the LORD?
 And who shall stand in his holy place?
He who has clean hands and a pure heart,
 who does not lift up his soul to what is false
 and does not swear deceitfully.
He will receive blessing from the LORD
 and righteousness from the God of his salvation.
Such is the generation of those who seek him,
 who seek the face of the God of Jacob. Selah

Lift up your heads, O gates!
 And be lifted up, O ancient doors,
 that the King of glory may come in.
Who is this King of glory?
 The LORD, strong and mighty,
 the LORD, mighty in battle!
Lift up your heads, O gates!
 And lift them up, O ancient doors,
 that the King of glory may come in.
Who is this King of glory?
 The LORD of hosts,
 he is the King of glory! Selah

Psalm 25

A request for instruction from the Lord, the redeemer and teacher of righteousness.

To you, O LORD, I lift up my soul.
O my God, in you I trust;
 let me not be put to shame;
 let not my enemies exult over me.

Indeed, none who wait for you shall be put to shame;
    they shall be ashamed who are wantonly treacherous.

Make me to know your ways, O LORD;
    teach me your paths.
Lead me in your truth and teach me,
    for you are the God of my salvation;
    for you I wait all the day long.

Remember your mercy, O LORD, and your steadfast love,
    for they have been from of old.
Remember not the sins of my youth or my transgressions;
    according to your steadfast love remember me,
    for the sake of your goodness, O LORD!

Good and upright is the LORD;
    therefore he instructs sinners in the way.
He leads the humble in what is right,
    and teaches the humble his way.
All the paths of the LORD are steadfast love and faithfulness,
    for those who keep his covenant and his testimonies.

For your name's sake, O LORD,
    pardon my guilt, for it is great.
Who is the man who fears the LORD?
    Him will he instruct in the way that he should choose.
His soul shall abide in well-being,
    and his offspring shall inherit the land.
The friendship of the LORD is for those who fear him,
    and he makes known to them his covenant.
My eyes are ever toward the LORD,
    for he will pluck my feet out of the net.

Turn to me and be gracious to me,
    for I am lonely and afflicted.
The troubles of my heart are enlarged;
    bring me out of my distresses.
Consider my affliction and my trouble,
    and forgive all my sins.

Consider how many are my foes,
    and with what violent hatred they hate me.
Oh, guard my soul, and deliver me!
    Let me not be put to shame, for I take refuge in you.
May integrity and uprightness preserve me,
    for I wait for you.

Redeem Israel, O God,
    out of all his troubles.

Psalm 27

With God on my side I have nothing to fear.

The LORD is my light and my salvation;
    whom shall I fear?
The LORD is the stronghold of my life;
    of whom shall I be afraid?

When evildoers assail me
    to eat up my flesh,
my adversaries and foes,
    it is they who stumble and fall.

Though an army encamp against me,
    my heart shall not fear;

though war arise against me,
yet I will be confident.

One thing have I asked of the LORD,
that will I seek after:
that I may dwell in the house of the LORD
all the days of my life,
to gaze upon the beauty of the LORD
and to inquire in his temple.

For he will hide me in his shelter
in the day of trouble;
he will conceal me under the cover of his tent;
he will lift me high upon a rock.

And now my head shall be lifted up
above my enemies all around me,
and I will offer in his tent
sacrifices with shouts of joy;
I will sing and make melody to the LORD.

Hear, O LORD, when I cry aloud;
be gracious to me and answer me!
You have said, "Seek my face."
My heart says to you,
"Your face, LORD, do I seek."
Hide not your face from me.
Turn not your servant away in anger,
O you who have been my help.
Cast me not off; forsake me not,
O God of my salvation!

For my father and my mother have forsaken me,
  but the LORD will take me in.

Teach me your way, O LORD,
  and lead me on a level path
  because of my enemies.
Give me not up to the will of my adversaries;
  for false witnesses have risen against me,
  and they breathe out violence.

I believe that I shall look upon the goodness of the LORD
  in the land of the living!
Wait for the LORD;
  be strong, and let your heart take courage;
  wait for the LORD!

Psalm 29

Worship the Lord in his glory and splendor.

Ascribe to the LORD, O heavenly beings,
  ascribe to the LORD glory and strength.
Ascribe to the LORD the glory due his name;
  worship the LORD in the splendor of holiness.

The voice of the LORD is over the waters;
  the God of glory thunders,
  the LORD, over many waters.
The voice of the LORD is powerful;
  the voice of the LORD is full of majesty.

The voice of the LORD breaks the cedars;
  the LORD breaks the cedars of Lebanon.

He makes Lebanon to skip like a calf,
  and Sirion like a young wild ox.

The voice of the LORD flashes forth flames of fire.
The voice of the LORD shakes the wilderness;
  the LORD shakes the wilderness of Kadesh.

The voice of the LORD makes the deer give birth
  and strips the forests bare,
  and in his temple all cry, "Glory!"

The LORD sits enthroned over the flood;
  the LORD sits enthroned as king forever.
May the LORD give strength to his people!
  May the LORD bless his people with peace!

PSALM 32

There is blessing in the confession and forgiveness of sin.

Blessed is the one whose transgression is forgiven,
  whose sin is covered.
Blessed is the man against whom the LORD counts no iniquity,
  and in whose spirit there is no deceit.

For when I kept silent, my bones wasted away
  through my groaning all day long.
For day and night your hand was heavy upon me;
  my strength was dried up as by the heat of summer. Selah

I acknowledged my sin to you,
  and I did not cover my iniquity;

I said, "I will confess my transgressions to the LORD,"
>*and you forgave the iniquity of my sin. Selah*

Therefore let everyone who is godly
>*offer prayer to you at a time when you may be found;*
surely in the rush of great waters,
>*they shall not reach him.*
You are a hiding place for me;
>*you preserve me from trouble;*
>*you surround me with shouts of deliverance. Selah*

I will instruct you and teach you in the way you should go;
>*I will counsel you with my eye upon you.*
Be not like a horse or a mule, without understanding,
>*which must be curbed with bit and bridle,*
>*or it will not stay near you.*

Many are the sorrows of the wicked,
>*but steadfast love surrounds the one who trusts in the LORD.*
Be glad in the LORD, and rejoice, O righteous,
>*and shout for joy, all you upright in heart!*

PSALM 34

God will provide for all those who seek and fear him.

I will bless the LORD at all times;
>*his praise shall continually be in my mouth.*
My soul makes its boast in the LORD;
>*let the humble hear and be glad.*
Oh, magnify the LORD with me,
>*and let us exalt his name together!*

Book One

I sought the LORD, and he answered me
    and delivered me from all my fears.
Those who look to him are radiant,
    and their faces shall never be ashamed.
This poor man cried, and the LORD heard him
    and saved him out of all his troubles.
The angel of the LORD encamps
    around those who fear him, and delivers them.

Oh, taste and see that the LORD is good!
    Blessed is the man who takes refuge in him!
Oh, fear the LORD, you his saints,
    for those who fear him have no lack!
The young lions suffer want and hunger;
    but those who seek the LORD lack no good thing.

Come, O children, listen to me;
    I will teach you the fear of the LORD.
What man is there who desires life
    and loves many days, that he may see good?
Keep your tongue from evil
    and your lips from speaking deceit.
Turn away from evil and do good;
    seek peace and pursue it.

The eyes of the LORD are toward the righteous
    and his ears toward their cry.
The face of the LORD is against those who do evil,
    to cut off the memory of them from the earth.
When the righteous cry for help, the LORD hears
    and delivers them out of all their troubles.

The LORD is near to the brokenhearted
    and saves the crushed in spirit.

Many are the afflictions of the righteous,
    but the LORD delivers him out of them all.
He keeps all his bones;
    not one of them is broken.
Affliction will slay the wicked,
    and those who hate the righteous will be condemned.
The LORD redeems the life of his servants;
    none of those who take refuge in him will be condemned.

Psalm 36

The steadfast love of God spans the universe and is a shield to his children.

Transgression speaks to the wicked
    deep in his heart;
there is no fear of God
    before his eyes.
For he flatters himself in his own eyes
    that his iniquity cannot be found out and hated.
The words of his mouth are trouble and deceit;
    he has ceased to act wisely and do good.
He plots trouble while on his bed;
    he sets himself in a way that is not good;
    he does not reject evil.

Your steadfast love, O LORD, extends to the heavens,
    your faithfulness to the clouds.
Your righteousness is like the mountains of God;
    your judgments are like the great deep;
    man and beast you save, O LORD.

How precious is your steadfast love, O God!
> *The children of mankind take refuge in the shadow of*
>> *your wings.*
They feast on the abundance of your house,
> *and you give them drink from the river of your delights.*
For with you is the fountain of life;
> *in your light do we see light.*

Oh, continue your steadfast love to those who know you,
> *and your righteousness to the upright of heart!*
Let not the foot of arrogance come upon me,
> *nor the hand of the wicked drive me away.*
There the evildoers lie fallen;
> *they are thrust down, unable to rise.*

PSALM 37
Wait on the Lord and he will show himself faithful.

Fret not yourself because of evildoers;
> *be not envious of wrongdoers!*
For they will soon fade like the grass
> *and wither like the green herb.*

Trust in the LORD, and do good;
> *dwell in the land and befriend faithfulness.*
Delight yourself in the LORD,
> *and he will give you the desires of your heart.*

Commit your way to the LORD;
> *trust in him, and he will act.*
He will bring forth your righteousness as the light,
> *and your justice as the noonday.*

Psalms

Be still before the LORD and wait patiently for him;
>> fret not yourself over the one who prospers in his way,
>> over the man who carries out evil devices!

Refrain from anger, and forsake wrath!
>> Fret not yourself; it tends only to evil.
For the evildoers shall be cut off,
>> but those who wait for the LORD shall inherit the land.

In just a little while, the wicked will be no more;
>> though you look carefully at his place, he will not be there.
But the meek shall inherit the land
>> and delight themselves in abundant peace.

The wicked plots against the righteous
>> and gnashes his teeth at him,
but the Lord laughs at the wicked,
>> for he sees that his day is coming.

The wicked draw the sword and bend their bows
>> to bring down the poor and needy,
>> to slay those whose way is upright;
their sword shall enter their own heart,
>> and their bows shall be broken.

Better is the little that the righteous has
>> than the abundance of many wicked.
For the arms of the wicked shall be broken,
>> but the LORD upholds the righteous.

The LORD knows the days of the blameless,
>> and their heritage will remain forever;

they are not put to shame in evil times;
  in the days of famine they have abundance.

But the wicked will perish;
  the enemies of the LORD are like the glory of the pastures;
  they vanish—like smoke they vanish away.

The wicked borrows but does not pay back,
  but the righteous is generous and gives;
for those blessed by the LORD shall inherit the land,
  but those cursed by him shall be cut off.

The steps of a man are established by the LORD,
  when he delights in his way;
though he fall, he shall not be cast headlong,
  for the LORD upholds his hand.

I have been young, and now am old,
  yet I have not seen the righteous forsaken
  or his children begging for bread.
He is ever lending generously,
  and his children become a blessing.

Turn away from evil and do good;
  so shall you dwell forever.
For the LORD loves justice;
  he will not forsake his saints.
They are preserved forever,
  but the children of the wicked shall be cut off.
The righteous shall inherit the land
  and dwell upon it forever.

Psalms

The mouth of the righteous utters wisdom,
 and his tongue speaks justice.
The law of his God is in his heart;
 his steps do not slip.

The wicked watches for the righteous
 and seeks to put him to death.
The LORD will not abandon him to his power
 or let him be condemned when he is brought to trial.

Wait for the LORD and keep his way,
 and he will exalt you to inherit the land;
 you will look on when the wicked are cut off.

I have seen a wicked, ruthless man,
 spreading himself like a green laurel tree.
But he passed away, and behold, he was no more;
 though I sought him, he could not be found.

Mark the blameless and behold the upright,
 for there is a future for the man of peace.
But transgressors shall be altogether destroyed;
 the future of the wicked shall be cut off.

The salvation of the righteous is from the LORD;
 he is their stronghold in the time of trouble.
The LORD helps them and delivers them;
 he delivers them from the wicked and saves them,
 because they take refuge in him.

BOOK TWO

PSALM 42

**An earnest expression of longing for God in the midst of
deep distress.**

As a deer pants for flowing streams,
*   so pants my soul for you, O God.*
My soul thirsts for God,
*   for the living God.*
When shall I come and appear before God?
My tears have been my food
*   day and night,*
while they say to me all the day long,
*   "Where is your God?"*
These things I remember,
*   as I pour out my soul:*
how I would go with the throng
*   and lead them in procession to the house of God*
with glad shouts and songs of praise,
*   a multitude keeping festival.*

Why are you cast down, O my soul,
*   and why are you in turmoil within me?*
Hope in God; for I shall again praise him,
*   my salvation and my God.*

My soul is cast down within me;
*   therefore I remember you*
from the land of Jordan and of Hermon,
*   from Mount Mizar.*

Deep calls to deep
> *at the roar of your waterfalls;*
all your breakers and your waves
> *have gone over me.*
By day the LORD commands his steadfast love,
> *and at night his song is with me,*
> *a prayer to the God of my life.*
I say to God, my rock:
> *"Why have you forgotten me?*
Why do I go mourning
> *because of the oppression of the enemy?"*
As with a deadly wound in my bones,
> *my adversaries taunt me,*
while they say to me all the day long,
> *"Where is your God?"*

Why are you cast down, O my soul,
> *and why are you in turmoil within me?*
Hope in God; for I shall again praise him,
> *my salvation and my God.*

PSALM 43

God defends and justifies the righteous person who cries to him.

Vindicate me, O God, and defend my cause
> *against an ungodly people,*
from the deceitful and unjust man
> *deliver me!*
For you are the God in whom I take refuge;
> *why have you rejected me?*
Why do I go about mourning
> *because of the oppression of the enemy?*

Send out your light and your truth;
    let them lead me;
let them bring me to your holy hill
    and to your dwelling!
Then I will go to the altar of God,
    to God my exceeding joy,
and I will praise you with the lyre,
    O God, my God.

Why are you cast down, O my soul,
    and why are you in turmoil within me?
Hope in God; for I shall again praise him,
    my salvation and my God.

PSALM 45

In celebration of the wedding of the King and his bride.

My heart overflows with a pleasing theme;
    I address my verses to the king;
    my tongue is like the pen of a ready scribe.

You are the most handsome of the sons of men;
    grace is poured upon your lips;
    therefore God has blessed you forever.
Gird your sword on your thigh, O mighty one,
    in your splendor and majesty!

In your majesty ride out victoriously
    for the cause of truth and meekness and righteousness;
    let your right hand teach you awesome deeds!
Your arrows are sharp
    in the heart of the king's enemies;
    the peoples fall under you.

Your throne, O God, is forever and ever.
> *The scepter of your kingdom is a scepter of*
>> *uprightness;*
> *you have loved righteousness and hated wickedness.*

Therefore God, your God, has anointed you
> *with the oil of gladness beyond your companions;*
> *your robes are all fragrant with myrrh and aloes and*
>> *cassia.*

From ivory palaces stringed instruments make
> *you glad;*
> *daughters of kings are among your ladies of honor;*
> *at your right hand stands the queen in gold of Ophir.*

Hear, O daughter, and consider, and incline your ear:
> *forget your people and your father's house,*
> *and the king will desire your beauty.*

Since he is your lord, bow to him.
> *The people of Tyre will seek your favor with gifts,*
> *the richest of the people.*

All glorious is the princess in her chamber, with robes interwoven
>> *with gold.*
> *In many-colored robes she is led to the king,*
> *with her virgin companions following behind her.*

With joy and gladness they are led along
> *as they enter the palace of the king.*

In place of your fathers shall be your sons;
> *you will make them princes in all the earth.*

I will cause your name to be remembered in all generations;
> *therefore nations will praise you forever and ever.*

Psalm 46

Even in the midst of turmoil and disaster, the people of God have nothing to fear.

God is our refuge and strength,
>> *a very present help in trouble.*
Therefore we will not fear though the earth gives way,
>> *though the mountains be moved into the heart*
>>> *of the sea,*
though its waters roar and foam,
>> *though the mountains tremble at its swelling. Selah*

There is a river whose streams make glad the
>> *city of God,*
>> *the holy habitation of the Most High.*
God is in the midst of her; she shall not be moved;
>> *God will help her when morning dawns.*
The nations rage, the kingdoms totter;
>> *he utters his voice, the earth melts.*
The Lord of hosts is with us;
>> *the God of Jacob is our fortress. Selah*

Come, behold the works of the Lord,
>> *how he has brought desolations on the earth.*
He makes wars cease to the end of the earth;
>> *he breaks the bow and shatters the spear;*
>> *he burns the chariots with fire.*
"Be still, and know that I am God.
>> *I will be exalted among the nations,*
>> *I will be exalted in the earth!"*
The Lord of hosts is with us;
>> *the God of Jacob is our fortress. Selah*

PSALM 47

Give praise to God, the King and ruler over all nations.

Clap your hands, all peoples!
    Shout to God with loud songs of joy!
For the LORD, the Most High, is to be feared,
    a great king over all the earth.
He subdued peoples under us,
    and nations under our feet.
He chose our heritage for us,
    the pride of Jacob whom he loves. Selah

God has gone up with a shout,
    the LORD with the sound of a trumpet.
Sing praises to God, sing praises!
    Sing praises to our King, sing praises!
For God is the King of all the earth;
    sing praises with a psalm!

God reigns over the nations;
    God sits on his holy throne.
The princes of the peoples gather
    as the people of the God of Abraham.
For the shields of the earth belong to God;
    he is highly exalted!

PSALM 48

God is great in Zion, and the city is safe under his watch.

Great is the LORD and greatly to be praised
    in the city of our God!
His holy mountain, beautiful in elevation,
    is the joy of all the earth,

Book Two

Mount Zion, in the far north,
       the city of the great King.
Within her citadels God
       has made himself known as a fortress.

For behold, the kings assembled;
       they came on together.
As soon as they saw it, they were astounded;
       they were in panic; they took to flight.
Trembling took hold of them there,
       anguish as of a woman in labor.
By the east wind you shattered
       the ships of Tarshish.
As we have heard, so have we seen
       in the city of the LORD of hosts,
in the city of our God,
       which God will establish forever. Selah

We have thought on your steadfast love, O God,
       in the midst of your temple.
As your name, O God,
       so your praise reaches to the ends of the earth.
Your right hand is filled with righteousness.
       Let Mount Zion be glad!
Let the daughters of Judah rejoice
       because of your judgments!

Walk about Zion, go around her,
       number her towers,
consider well her ramparts,
       go through her citadels,
that you may tell the next generation

that this is God,
our God forever and ever.
He will guide us forever.

Psalm 49

A lesson in stewardship: great riches cannot provide eternal security.

Hear this, all peoples!
Give ear, all inhabitants of the world,
both low and high,
rich and poor together!
My mouth shall speak wisdom;
the meditation of my heart shall be understanding.
I will incline my ear to a proverb;
I will solve my riddle to the music of the lyre.

Why should I fear in times of trouble,
when the iniquity of those who cheat me surrounds me,
those who trust in their wealth
and boast of the abundance of their riches?
Truly no man can ransom another,
or give to God the price of his life,
for the ransom of their life is costly
and can never suffice,
that he should live on forever
and never see the pit.

For he sees that even the wise die;
the fool and the stupid alike must perish
and leave their wealth to others.
Their graves are their homes forever,
their dwelling places to all generations,

though they called lands by their own names.
Man in his pomp will not remain;
    he is like the beasts that perish.

This is the path of those who have foolish confidence;
    yet after them people approve of their boasts. Selah
Like sheep they are appointed for Sheol;
    death shall be their shepherd,
and the upright shall rule over them in the morning.
    Their form shall be consumed in Sheol, with no place to dwell.
But God will ransom my soul from the power of Sheol,
    for he will receive me. Selah

Be not afraid when a man becomes rich,
    when the glory of his house increases.
For when he dies he will carry nothing away;
    his glory will not go down after him.
For though, while he lives, he counts himself blessed
    —and though you get praise when you do well for yourself—
his soul will go to the generation of his fathers,
    who will never again see light.
Man in his pomp yet without understanding is like the beasts that
    perish.

PSALM 51

A humble plea for the mercy and forgiveness of God.

Have mercy on me, O God,
    according to your steadfast love;
according to your abundant mercy
    blot out my transgressions.
Wash me thoroughly from my iniquity,
    and cleanse me from my sin!

Psalms

For I know my transgressions,
    and my sin is ever before me.
Against you, you only, have I sinned
    and done what is evil in your sight,
so that you may be justified in your words
    and blameless in your judgment.
Behold, I was brought forth in iniquity,
    and in sin did my mother conceive me.
Behold, you delight in truth in the inward being,
    and you teach me wisdom in the secret heart.

Purge me with hyssop, and I shall be clean;
    wash me, and I shall be whiter than snow.
Let me hear joy and gladness;
    let the bones that you have broken rejoice.
Hide your face from my sins,
    and blot out all my iniquities.
Create in me a clean heart, O God,
    and renew a right spirit within me.
Cast me not away from your presence,
    and take not your Holy Spirit from me.
Restore to me the joy of your salvation,
    and uphold me with a willing spirit.

Then I will teach transgressors your ways,
    and sinners will return to you.
Deliver me from bloodguiltiness, O God,
        O God of my salvation,
    and my tongue will sing aloud of your righteousness.
O Lord, open my lips,
    and my mouth will declare your praise.
For you will not delight in sacrifice, or I would give it;

you will not be pleased with a burnt offering.
The sacrifices of God are a broken spirit;
a broken and contrite heart, O God, you will not despise.

Do good to Zion in your good pleasure;
build up the walls of Jerusalem;
then will you delight in right sacrifices,
in burnt offerings and whole burnt offerings;
then bulls will be offered on your altar.

PSALM 52

A confident declaration that God will bring justice to bear on those who practice *evil.*

Why do you boast of evil, O mighty man?
The steadfast love of God endures all the day.
Your tongue plots destruction,
like a sharp razor, you worker of deceit.
You love evil more than good,
and lying more than speaking what is right. Selah
You love all words that devour,
O deceitful tongue.

But God will break you down forever;
he will snatch and tear you from your tent;
he will uproot you from the land of the living. Selah
The righteous shall see and fear,
and shall laugh at him, saying,
"See the man who would not make
God his refuge,
but trusted in the abundance of his riches
and sought refuge in his own destruction!"

But I am like a green olive tree
    in the house of God.
I trust in the steadfast love of God
    forever and ever.
I will thank you forever,
    because you have done it.
I will wait for your name, for it is good,
    in the presence of the godly.

Psalm 55

Come to my aid: a prayer for God's help in the face of a mighty enemy.

Give ear to my prayer, O God,
    and hide not yourself from my plea for mercy!
Attend to me, and answer me;
    I am restless in my complaint and I moan,
because of the noise of the enemy,
    because of the oppression of the wicked.
For they drop trouble upon me,
    and in anger they bear a grudge against me.

My heart is in anguish within me;
    the terrors of death have fallen upon me.
Fear and trembling come upon me,
    and horror overwhelms me.
And I say, "Oh, that I had wings like a dove!
    I would fly away and be at rest;
yes, I would wander far away;
    I would lodge in the wilderness; Selah
I would hurry to find a shelter
    from the raging wind and tempest."

Book Two

Destroy, O Lord, divide their tongues;
>for I see violence and strife in the city.
Day and night they go around it
>on its walls,
and iniquity and trouble are within it;
>ruin is in its midst;
oppression and fraud
>do not depart from its marketplace.

For it is not an enemy who taunts me—
>then I could bear it;
it is not an adversary who deals insolently with me—
>then I could hide from him.
But it is you, a man, my equal,
>my companion, my familiar friend.
We used to take sweet counsel together;
>within God's house we walked in the throng.
Let death steal over them;
>let them go down to Sheol alive;
>for evil is in their dwelling place and in their heart.

But I call to God,
>and the LORD will save me.
Evening and morning and at noon
>I utter my complaint and moan,
>and he hears my voice.
He redeems my soul in safety
>from the battle that I wage,
>for many are arrayed against me.
God will give ear and humble them,
>he who is enthroned from of old, Selah

because they do not change
     and do not fear God.

My companion stretched out his hand against his friends;
     he violated his covenant.
His speech was smooth as butter,
     yet war was in his heart;
his words were softer than oil,
     yet they were drawn swords.

Cast your burden on the LORD,
     and he will sustain you;
he will never permit
     the righteous to be moved.

But you, O God, will cast them down
     into the pit of destruction;
men of blood and treachery
     shall not live out half their days.
But I will trust in you.

PSALM 56

A statement of faith in God, despite an enemy's attack.

Be gracious to me, O God, for man tramples on me;
     all day long an attacker oppresses me;
my enemies trample on me all day long,
     for many attack me proudly.
When I am afraid,
     I put my trust in you.
In God, whose word I praise,
     in God I trust; I shall not be afraid.
     What can flesh do to me?

All day long they injure my cause;
>   all their thoughts are against me for evil.
They stir up strife, they lurk;
>   they watch my steps,
>   as they have waited for my life.
For their crime will they escape?
>   In wrath cast down the peoples, O God!

You have kept count of my tossings;
>   put my tears in your bottle.
>   Are they not in your book?
Then my enemies will turn back
>   in the day when I call.
>   This I know, that God is for me.
In God, whose word I praise,
>   in the LORD, whose word I praise,
in God I trust; I shall not be afraid.
>   What can man do to me?

I must perform my vows to you, O God;
>   I will render thank offerings to you.
For you have delivered my soul from death,
>   yes, my feet from falling,
that I may walk before God
>   in the light of life.

PSALM 57

Until the danger passes: a testimony to the refuge God affords in the midst of trouble.

Be merciful to me, O God, be merciful to me,
>   for in you my soul takes refuge;
in the shadow of your wings I will take refuge,

till the storms of destruction pass by.
I cry out to God Most High,
    to God who fulfills his purpose for me.
He will send from heaven and save me;
    he will put to shame him who tramples on me. Selah
God will send out his steadfast love and his faithfulness!

My soul is in the midst of lions;
    I lie down amid fiery beasts—
the children of man, whose teeth are spears and arrows,
    whose tongues are sharp swords.

Be exalted, O God, above the heavens!
    Let your glory be over all the earth!

They set a net for my steps;
    my soul was bowed down.
They dug a pit in my way,
    but they have fallen into it themselves. Selah
My heart is steadfast, O God,
    my heart is steadfast!
I will sing and make melody!
    Awake, my glory!
Awake, O harp and lyre!
    I will awake the dawn!
I will give thanks to you, O Lord, among the peoples;
    I will sing praises to you among the nations.
For your steadfast love is great to the heavens,
    your faithfulness to the clouds.

Be exalted, O God, above the heavens!
    Let your glory be over all the earth!

PSALM 60

A lament for a nation and a cry for the restoration of God.

O God, you have rejected us, broken our defenses;
    you have been angry; oh, restore us.
You have made the land to quake; you have torn it open;
    repair its breaches, for it totters.
You have made your people see hard things;
    you have given us wine to drink that made us stagger.

You have set up a banner for those who fear you,
    that they may flee to it from the bow. Selah
That your beloved ones may be delivered,
    give salvation by your right hand and answer us!

God has spoken in his holiness:
    "With exultation I will divide up Shechem
    and portion out the Vale of Succoth.
Gilead is mine; Manasseh is mine;
    Ephraim is my helmet;
    Judah is my scepter.
Moab is my washbasin;
    upon Edom I cast my shoe;
    over Philistia I shout in triumph."

Who will bring me to the fortified city?
    Who will lead me to Edom?
Have you not rejected us, O God?
    You do not go forth, O God, with our armies.
Oh, grant us help against the foe,
    for vain is the salvation of man!

With God we shall do valiantly;
>> it is he who will tread down our foes.

Psalm 63

A desperate confession of the need to be in God's presence.

O God, you are my God; earnestly I seek you;
>> my soul thirsts for you;
my flesh faints for you,
>> as in a dry and weary land where there is no water.
So I have looked upon you in the sanctuary,
>> beholding your power and glory.
Because your steadfast love is better than life,
>> my lips will praise you.
So I will bless you as long as I live;
>> in your name I will lift up my hands.

My soul will be satisfied as with fat and rich food,
>> and my mouth will praise you with joyful lips,
when I remember you upon my bed,
>> and meditate on you in the watches of the night;
for you have been my help,
>> and in the shadow of your wings I will sing for joy.
My soul clings to you;
>> your right hand upholds me.

But those who seek to destroy my life
>> shall go down into the depths of the earth;
they shall be given over to the power of the sword;
>> they shall be a portion for jackals.
But the king shall rejoice in God;

all who swear by him shall exult,
    for the mouths of liars will be stopped.

PSALM 71

In my weakness: a plea for God's deliverance.

In you, O LORD, do I take refuge;
    let me never be put to shame!
In your righteousness deliver me and rescue me;
    incline your ear to me, and save me!
Be to me a rock of refuge,
    to which I may continually come;
you have given the command to save me,
    for you are my rock and my fortress.

Rescue me, O my God, from the hand of the wicked,
    from the grasp of the unjust and cruel man.
For you, O Lord, are my hope,
    my trust, O LORD, from my youth.
Upon you I have leaned from before my birth;
    you are he who took me from my mother's womb.
My praise is continually of you.

I have been as a portent to many,
    but you are my strong refuge.
My mouth is filled with your praise,
    and with your glory all the day.
Do not cast me off in the time of old age;
    forsake me not when my strength is spent.
For my enemies speak concerning me;
    those who watch for my life consult together
and say, "God has forsaken him;

pursue and seize him,
for there is none to deliver him."

O God, be not far from me;
O my God, make haste to help me!
May my accusers be put to shame and consumed;
with scorn and disgrace may they be covered
who seek my hurt.
But I will hope continually
and will praise you yet more and more.
My mouth will tell of your righteous acts,
of your deeds of salvation all the day,
for their number is past my knowledge.
With the mighty deeds of the Lord God I will come;
I will remind them of your righteousness, yours alone.

O God, from my youth you have taught me,
and I still proclaim your wondrous deeds.
So even to old age and gray hairs,
O God, do not forsake me,
until I proclaim your might to another generation,
your power to all those to come.
Your righteousness, O God,
reaches the high heavens.
You who have done great things,
O God, who is like you?
You who have made me see many troubles and calamities
will revive me again;
from the depths of the earth
you will bring me up again.
You will increase my greatness
and comfort me again.

I will also praise you with the harp
>   for your faithfulness, O my God;
I will sing praises to you with the lyre,
>   O Holy One of Israel.
My lips will shout for joy,
>   when I sing praises to you;
>   my soul also, which you have redeemed.
And my tongue will talk of your righteous help
>   all the day long,
for they have been put to shame and disappointed
>   who sought to do me hurt.

PSALM 72

Lifting up a leader: a prayer for the king.

Give the king your justice, O God,
>   and your righteousness to the royal son!
May he judge your people with righteousness,
>   and your poor with justice!
Let the mountains bear prosperity for the people,
>   and the hills, in righteousness!
May he defend the cause of the poor of the people,
>   give deliverance to the children of the needy,
>   and crush the oppressor!

May they fear you while the sun endures,
>   and as long as the moon, throughout all generations!
May he be like rain that falls on the mown grass,
>   like showers that water the earth!
In his days may the righteous flourish,
>   and peace abound, till the moon be no more!

Psalms

May he have dominion from sea to sea,
  and from the River to the ends of the earth!
May desert tribes bow down before him,
  and his enemies lick the dust!
May the kings of Tarshish and of the coastlands
  render him tribute;
may the kings of Sheba and Seba
  bring gifts!
May all kings fall down before him,
  all nations serve him!

For he delivers the needy when he calls,
  the poor and him who has no helper.
He has pity on the weak and the needy,
  and saves the lives of the needy.
From oppression and violence he redeems their life,
  and precious is their blood in his sight.

Long may he live;
  may gold of Sheba be given to him!
May prayer be made for him continually,
  and blessings invoked for him all the day!
May there be abundance of grain in the land;
  on the tops of the mountains may it wave;
  may its fruit be like Lebanon;
and may people blossom in the cities
  like the grass of the field!
May his name endure forever,
  his fame continue as long as the sun!
May people be blessed in him,
  all nations call him blessed!

Book Two

Blessed be the LORD, the God of Israel,
*   who alone does wondrous things.*
Blessed be his glorious name forever;
*   may the whole earth be filled with his glory!*
*   Amen and Amen!*

BOOK THREE

PSALM 73

It is better to face difficulties with righteousness than to prosper in wickedness.

Truly God is good to Israel,
*   to those who are pure in heart.*
But as for me, my feet had almost stumbled,
*   my steps had nearly slipped.*
For I was envious of the arrogant
*   when I saw the prosperity of the wicked.*

For they have no pangs until death;
*   their bodies are fat and sleek.*
They are not in trouble as others are;
*   they are not stricken like the rest of mankind.*
Therefore pride is their necklace;
*   violence covers them as a garment.*
Their eyes swell out through fatness;
*   their hearts overflow with follies.*
They scoff and speak with malice;
*   loftily they threaten oppression.*
They set their mouths against the heavens,
*   and their tongue struts through the earth.*
Therefore his people turn back to them,
*   and find no fault in them.*
And they say, "How can God know?
*   Is there knowledge in the Most High?"*
Behold, these are the wicked;
*   always at ease, they increase in riches.*

Book Three

All in vain have I kept my heart clean
       and washed my hands in innocence.
For all the day long I have been stricken
       and rebuked every morning.
If I had said, "I will speak thus,"
       I would have betrayed the generation of your children.

But when I thought how to understand this,
       it seemed to me a wearisome task,
until I went into the sanctuary of God;
       then I discerned their end.

Truly you set them in slippery places;
       you make them fall to ruin.
How they are destroyed in a moment,
       swept away utterly by terrors!
Like a dream when one awakes,
       O Lord, when you rouse yourself, you despise them
              as phantoms.
When my soul was embittered,
       when I was pricked in heart,
I was brutish and ignorant;
       I was like a beast toward you.

Nevertheless, I am continually with you;
       you hold my right hand.
You guide me with your counsel,
       and afterward you will receive me to glory.
Whom have I in heaven but you?
       And there is nothing on earth that I desire besides you.
My flesh and my heart may fail,
       but God is the strength of my heart and my portion forever.

For behold, those who are far from you shall perish;
you put an end to everyone who is unfaithful to you.
But for me it is good to be near God;
I have made the Lord GOD my refuge,
that I may tell of all your works.

PSALM 75

God is in control; he will humble the arrogant and silence the wicked.

We give thanks to you, O God;
we give thanks, for your name is near.
We recount your wondrous deeds.

"At the set time that I appoint
I will judge with equity.
When the earth totters, and all its inhabitants,
it is I who keep steady its pillars. Selah
I say to the boastful, 'Do not boast,'
and to the wicked, 'Do not lift up your horn;
do not lift up your horn on high,
or speak with haughty neck.'"

For not from the east or from the west
and not from the wilderness comes lifting up,
but it is God who executes judgment,
putting down one and lifting up another.
For in the hand of the LORD there is a cup
with foaming wine, well mixed,
and he pours out from it,
and all the wicked of the earth
shall drain it down to the dregs.

But I will declare it forever;
>*I will sing praises to the God of Jacob.*
All the horns of the wicked I will cut off,
>*but the horns of the righteous shall be lifted up.*

PSALM 77

**A lament reflecting the distress of the present and
remembering the mercy of the** *past.*

I cry aloud to God,
>*aloud to God, and he will hear me.*
In the day of my trouble I seek the Lord;
>*in the night my hand is stretched out without wearying;*
>*my soul refuses to be comforted.*
When I remember God, I moan;
>*when I meditate, my spirit faints. Selah*

You hold my eyelids open;
>*I am so troubled that I cannot speak.*
I consider the days of old,
>*the years long ago.*
I said, "Let me remember my song in the night;
>*let me meditate in my heart."*
>*Then my spirit made a diligent search:*
"Will the Lord spurn forever,
>*and never again be favorable?*
Has his steadfast love forever ceased?
>*Are his promises at an end for all time?*
Has God forgotten to be gracious?
>*Has he in anger shut up his compassion?" Selah*

Then I said, "I will appeal to this,
>*to the years of the right hand of the Most High."*

I will remember the deeds of the LORD;
>> yes, I will remember your wonders of old.
I will ponder all your work,
>> and meditate on your mighty deeds.
Your way, O God, is holy.
>> What god is great like our God?
You are the God who works wonders;
>> you have made known your might among the peoples.
You with your arm redeemed your people,
>> the children of Jacob and Joseph. Selah

When the waters saw you, O God,
>> when the waters saw you, they were afraid;
>> indeed, the deep trembled.
The clouds poured out water;
>> the skies gave forth thunder;
>> your arrows flashed on every side.
The crash of your thunder was in the whirlwind;
>> your lightnings lighted up the world;
>> the earth trembled and shook.
Your way was through the sea,
>> your path through the great waters;
>> yet your footprints were unseen.
You led your people like a flock
>> by the hand of Moses and Aaron.

PSALM 82

God protects the helpless and judges their oppressors.

God has taken his place in the divine council;
>> in the midst of the gods he holds judgment:
"How long will you judge unjustly
>> and show partiality to the wicked? Selah

Give justice to the weak and the fatherless;
 maintain the right of the afflicted and the destitute.
Rescue the weak and the needy;
 deliver them from the hand of the wicked."

They have neither knowledge nor understanding,
 they walk about in darkness;
 all the foundations of the earth are shaken.

I said, "You are gods,
 sons of the Most High, all of you;
nevertheless, like men you shall die,
 and fall like any prince."

Arise, O God, judge the earth;
 for you shall inherit all the nations!

Psalm 84

An expression of desire to be in the Lord's house.

How lovely is your dwelling place,
 O LORD of hosts!
My soul longs, yes, faints
 for the courts of the LORD;
my heart and flesh sing for joy
 to the living God.

Even the sparrow finds a home,
 and the swallow a nest for herself,
 where she may lay her young,
at your altars, O LORD of hosts,
 my King and my God.

Blessed are those who dwell in your house,
*   ever singing your praise! Selah*

Blessed are those whose strength is in you,
*   in whose heart are the highways to Zion.*
As they go through the Valley of Baca
*   they make it a place of springs;*
*   the early rain also covers it with pools.*
They go from strength to strength;
*   each one appears before God in Zion.*

O LORD God of hosts, hear my prayer;
*   give ear, O God of Jacob! Selah*
Behold our shield, O God;
*   look on the face of your anointed!*

For a day in your courts is better
*   than a thousand elsewhere.*
I would rather be a doorkeeper in the house of my God
*   than dwell in the tents of wickedness.*
For the LORD God is a sun and shield;
*   the LORD bestows favor and honor.*
No good thing does he withhold
*   from those who walk uprightly.*
O LORD of hosts,
*   blessed is the one who trusts in you!*

PSALM 86

A cry for salvation from enemies who do not fear the Lord.

Incline your ear, O LORD, and answer me,
*   for I am poor and needy.*
Preserve my life, for I am godly;

save your servant, who trusts in you—you are my God.
Be gracious to me, O Lord,
     for to you do I cry all the day.
Gladden the soul of your servant,
     for to you, O Lord, do I lift up my soul.
For you, O Lord, are good and forgiving,
     abounding in steadfast love to all who call upon you.
Give ear, O Lord, to my prayer;
     listen to my plea for grace.
In the day of my trouble I call upon you,
     for you answer me.

There is none like you among the gods, O Lord,
     nor are there any works like yours.
All the nations you have made shall come
     and worship before you, O Lord,
     and shall glorify your name.
For you are great and do wondrous things;
     you alone are God.
Teach me your way, O Lord,
     that I may walk in your truth;
     unite my heart to fear your name.
I give thanks to you, O Lord my God, with my whole heart,
     and I will glorify your name forever.
For great is your steadfast love toward me;
     you have delivered my soul from the depths of Sheol.

O God, insolent men have risen up against me;
     a band of ruthless men seeks my life,
     and they do not set you before them.

PSALMS

But you, O Lord, are a God merciful and gracious,
  slow to anger and abounding in steadfast love and
    faithfulness.
Turn to me and be gracious to me;
  give your strength to your servant,
  and save the son of your maidservant.
Show me a sign of your favor,
  that those who hate me may see and be put to shame
  because you, LORD, have helped me and comforted me.

BOOK FOUR

PSALM 90

A plea for compassion from God, who has been a source both of refuge and of admonition.

Lord, you have been our dwelling place
    in all generations.
Before the mountains were brought forth,
    or ever you had formed the earth and the world,
    from everlasting to everlasting you are God.

You return man to dust
    and say, "Return, O children of man!"
For a thousand years in your sight
    are but as yesterday when it is past,
    or as a watch in the night.

You sweep them away as with a flood; they are like
      a dream,
    like grass that is renewed in the morning:
in the morning it flourishes and is renewed;
    in the evening it fades and withers.

For we are brought to an end by your anger;
    by your wrath we are dismayed.
You have set our iniquities before you,
    our secret sins in the light of your presence.

For all our days pass away under your wrath;
    we bring our years to an end like a sigh.

The years of our life are seventy,
or even by reason of strength eighty;
yet their span is but toil and trouble;
they are soon gone, and we fly away.
Who considers the power of your anger,
and your wrath according to the fear of you?

So teach us to number our days
that we may get a heart of wisdom.
Return, O LORD! How long?
Have pity on your servants!
Satisfy us in the morning with your steadfast love,
that we may rejoice and be glad all our days.
Make us glad for as many days as you have afflicted us,
and for as many years as we have seen evil.
Let your work be shown to your servants,
and your glorious power to their children.
Let the favor of the Lord our God be upon us,
and establish the work of our hands upon us;
yes, establish the work of our hands!

PSALM 91

Praise to God as deliverer and provider.

He who dwells in the shelter of the Most High
will abide in the shadow of the Almighty.
I will say to the LORD, "My refuge and my fortress,
my God, in whom I trust."

For he will deliver you from the snare of the fowler
and from the deadly pestilence.
He will cover you with his pinions,
and under his wings you will find refuge;

his faithfulness is a shield and buckler.
You will not fear the terror of the night,
        nor the arrow that flies by day,
nor the pestilence that stalks in darkness,
        nor the destruction that wastes at noonday.

A thousand may fall at your side,
        ten thousand at your right hand,
        but it will not come near you.
You will only look with your eyes
        and see the recompense of the wicked.

Because you have made the LORD *your dwelling place—*
        the Most High, who is my refuge—
no evil shall be allowed to befall you,
        no plague come near your tent.

For he will command his angels concerning you
        to guard you in all your ways.
On their hands they will bear you up,
        lest you strike your foot against a stone.
You will tread on the lion and the adder;
        the young lion and the serpent you will trample
                underfoot.

"Because he holds fast to me in love, I will deliver him;
        I will protect him, because he knows my name.
When he calls to me, I will answer him;
        I will be with him in trouble;
        I will rescue him and honor him.
With long life I will satisfy him
        and show him my salvation."

PSALM 92

A testimony to the righteousness of God.

It is good to give thanks to the LORD,
    to sing praises to your name, O Most High;
to declare your steadfast love in the morning,
    and your faithfulness by night,
to the music of the lute and the harp,
    to the melody of the lyre.
For you, O LORD, have made me glad by your work;
    at the works of your hands I sing for joy.

How great are your works, O LORD!
    Your thoughts are very deep!
The stupid man cannot know;
    the fool cannot understand this:
that though the wicked sprout like grass
    and all evildoers flourish,
they are doomed to destruction forever;
    but you, O LORD, are on high forever.
For behold, your enemies, O LORD,
    for behold, your enemies shall perish;
    all evildoers shall be scattered.

But you have exalted my horn like that of the wild ox;
    you have poured over me fresh oil.
My eyes have seen the downfall of my enemies;
    my ears have heard the doom of my evil assailants.

The righteous flourish like the palm tree
    and grow like a cedar in Lebanon.
They are planted in the house of the LORD;

they flourish in the courts of our God.
They still bear fruit in old age;
　　they are ever full of sap and green,
to declare that the LORD is upright;
　　he is my rock, and there is no unrighteousness in him.

PSALM 93

"Mightier than the waves": an exalting of the eternal majesty of God.

The LORD reigns; he is robed in majesty;
　　the LORD is robed; he has put on strength as his belt.
Yes, the world is established; it shall never be moved.
Your throne is established from of old;
　　you are from everlasting.

The floods have lifted up, O LORD,
　　the floods have lifted up their voice;
　　the floods lift up their roaring.
Mightier than the thunders of many waters,
　　mightier than the waves of the sea,
　　the LORD on high is mighty!

Your decrees are very trustworthy;
　　holiness befits your house,
　　O LORD, forevermore.

PSALM 94

A cry to God to judge the wicked and avenge the weak.

O LORD, God of vengeance,
　　O God of vengeance, shine forth!
Rise up, O judge of the earth;

repay to the proud what they deserve!
O LORD, *how long shall the wicked,*
    how long shall the wicked exult?
They pour out their arrogant words;
    all the evildoers boast.
They crush your people, O LORD,
    and afflict your heritage.
They kill the widow and the sojourner,
    and murder the fatherless;
and they say, "The LORD *does not see;*
    the God of Jacob does not perceive."

Understand, O dullest of the people!
    Fools, when will you be wise?
He who planted the ear, does he not hear?
He who formed the eye, does he not see?
He who disciplines the nations, does he not rebuke?
He who teaches man knowledge—
    the LORD—*knows the thoughts of man,*
    that they are but a breath.

Blessed is the man whom you discipline, O LORD,
    and whom you teach out of your law,
to give him rest from days of trouble,
    until a pit is dug for the wicked.
For the LORD *will not forsake his people;*
    he will not abandon his heritage;
for justice will return to the righteous,
    and all the upright in heart will follow it.

Who rises up for me against the wicked?
    Who stands up for me against evildoers?

If the LORD had not been my help,
>> my soul would soon have lived in the land of silence.
When I thought, "My foot slips,"
>> your steadfast love, O LORD, held me up.
When the cares of my heart are many,
>> your consolations cheer my soul.
Can wicked rulers be allied with you,
>> those who frame injustice by statute?
They band together against the life of the righteous
>> and condemn the innocent to death.
But the LORD has become my stronghold,
>> and my God the rock of my refuge.
He will bring back on them their iniquity
>> and wipe them out for their wickedness;
>> the LORD our God will wipe them out.

PSALM 95

A call to worship: a plea to lift up the glory of the Lord.

Oh come, let us sing to the LORD;
>> let us make a joyful noise to the rock of our salvation!
Let us come into his presence with thanksgiving;
>> let us make a joyful noise to him with songs of praise!
For the LORD is a great God,
>> and a great King above all gods.
In his hand are the depths of the earth;
>> the heights of the mountains are his also.
The sea is his, for he made it,
>> and his hands formed the dry land.

Oh come, let us worship and bow down;
>> let us kneel before the LORD, our Maker!
For he is our God,

and we are the people of his pasture,
>> and the sheep of his hand.
Today, if you hear his voice,
>> do not harden your hearts, as at Meribah,
>> as on the day at Massah in the wilderness,
when your fathers put me to the test
>> and put me to the proof, though they had seen my work.
For forty years I loathed that generation
>> and said, "They are a people who go astray in their heart,
>> and they have not known my ways."
Therefore I swore in my wrath,
>> "They shall not enter my rest."

PSALM 96

A song of praise: a call for all nations to give glory to God.

Oh sing to the LORD a new song;
>> sing to the LORD, all the earth!
Sing to the LORD, bless his name;
>> tell of his salvation from day to day.
Declare his glory among the nations,
>> his marvelous works among all the peoples!
For great is the LORD, and greatly to be praised;
>> he is to be feared above all gods.
For all the gods of the peoples are worthless idols,
>> but the LORD made the heavens.
Splendor and majesty are before him;
>> strength and beauty are in his sanctuary.

Ascribe to the LORD, O families of the peoples,
>> ascribe to the LORD glory and strength!

Ascribe to the LORD the glory due his name;
　　bring an offering, and come into his courts!
Worship the LORD in the splendor of holiness;
　　tremble before him, all the earth!

Say among the nations, "The LORD reigns!
　　Yes, the world is established; it shall never be moved;
　　he will judge the peoples with equity."

Let the heavens be glad, and let the earth rejoice;
　　let the sea roar, and all that fills it;
　　let the field exult, and everything in it!
Then shall all the trees of the forest sing for joy
　　before the LORD, for he comes,
　　for he comes to judge the earth.
He will judge the world in righteousness,
　　and the peoples in his faithfulness.

PSALM 100

A proclamation of gratitude to God for his goodness.

Make a joyful noise to the LORD, all the earth!
　　Serve the LORD with gladness!
　　Come into his presence with singing!

Know that the LORD, he is God!
　　It is he who made us, and we are his;
　　we are his people, and the sheep of his pasture.

Enter his gates with thanksgiving,
　　and his courts with praise!
　　Give thanks to him; bless his name!

For the LORD is good;
>>*his steadfast love endures forever,*
>>*and his faithfulness to all generations.*

PSALM 101

A ruler pledges to lead his people with integrity.

I will sing of steadfast love and justice;
>>*to you, O LORD, I will make music.*
I will ponder the way that is blameless.
>>*Oh when will you come to me?*
I will walk with integrity of heart
>>*within my house;*
I will not set before my eyes
>>*anything that is worthless.*
I hate the work of those who fall away;
>>*it shall not cling to me.*
A perverse heart shall be far from me;
>>*I will know nothing of evil.*

Whoever slanders his neighbor secretly
>>*I will destroy.*
Whoever has a haughty look and an arrogant heart
>>*I will not endure.*

I will look with favor on the faithful in the land,
>>*that they may dwell with me;*
he who walks in the way that is blameless
>>*shall minister to me.*

No one who practices deceit
>>*shall dwell in my house;*

no one who utters lies
    shall continue before my eyes.

Morning by morning I will destroy
    all the wicked in the land,
cutting off all the evildoers
    from the city of the LORD.

PSALM 103

The mercy of our Lord: a testimony to God's compassion.

Bless the LORD, *O my soul,*
    and all that is within me,
        bless his holy name!
Bless the LORD, *O my soul,*
    and forget not all his benefits,
who forgives all your iniquity,
    who heals all your diseases,
who redeems your life from the pit,
    who crowns you with steadfast love and mercy,
who satisfies you with good
    so that your youth is renewed like the eagle's.

The LORD *works righteousness*
    and justice for all who are oppressed.
He made known his ways to Moses,
    his acts to the people of Israel.
The LORD *is merciful and gracious,*
    slow to anger and abounding in steadfast love.
He will not always chide,
    nor will he keep his anger forever.

He does not deal with us according to our sins,
nor repay us according to our iniquities.
For as high as the heavens are above the earth,
so great is his steadfast love toward those who
fear him;
as far as the east is from the west,
so far does he remove our transgressions from us.
As a father shows compassion to his children,
so the LORD shows compassion to those who fear him.
For he knows our frame;
he remembers that we are dust.

As for man, his days are like grass;
he flourishes like a flower of the field;
for the wind passes over it, and it is gone,
and its place knows it no more.
But the steadfast love of the LORD is from everlasting
to everlasting on those who fear him,
and his righteousness to children's children,
to those who keep his covenant
and remember to do his commandments.
The LORD has established his throne in the heavens,
and his kingdom rules over all.

Bless the LORD, O you his angels,
you mighty ones who do his word,
obeying the voice of his word!
Bless the LORD, all his hosts,
his ministers, who do his will!
Bless the LORD, all his works,
in all places of his dominion.
Bless the LORD, O my soul!

Book Four

PSALM 106
In retrospect: a confession of the rebellious history of Israel.

Praise the LORD!
Oh give thanks to the LORD, for he is good,
    for his steadfast love endures forever!
Who can utter the mighty deeds of the LORD,
    or declare all his praise?
Blessed are they who observe justice,
    who do righteousness at all times!

Remember me, O LORD, when you show favor to your people;
    help me when you save them,
that I may look upon the prosperity of your chosen ones,
    that I may rejoice in the gladness of your nation,
    that I may glory with your inheritance.

Both we and our fathers have sinned;
    we have committed iniquity; we have done wickedness.
Our fathers, when they were in Egypt,
    did not consider your wondrous works;
they did not remember the abundance of your steadfast love,
    but rebelled by the sea, at the Red Sea.
Yet he saved them for his name's sake,
    that he might make known his mighty power.
He rebuked the Red Sea, and it became dry,
    and he led them through the deep as through a desert.
So he saved them from the hand of the foe
    and redeemed them from the power of the enemy.
And the waters covered their adversaries;
    not one of them was left.

Then they believed his words;
    they sang his praise.

But they soon forgot his works;
    they did not wait for his counsel.
But they had a wanton craving in the wilderness,
    and put God to the test in the desert;
he gave them what they asked,
    but sent a wasting disease among them.

When men in the camp were jealous of Moses
    and Aaron, the holy one of the LORD,
the earth opened and swallowed up Dathan,
    and covered the company of Abiram.
Fire also broke out in their company;
    the flame burned up the wicked.

They made a calf in Horeb
    and worshiped a metal image.
They exchanged the glory of God
    for the image of an ox that eats grass.
They forgot God, their Savior,
    who had done great things in Egypt,
wondrous works in the land of Ham,
    and awesome deeds by the Red Sea.
Therefore he said he would destroy them—
    had not Moses, his chosen one,
stood in the breach before him,
    to turn away his wrath from destroying them.

Then they despised the pleasant land,
    having no faith in his promise.

They murmured in their tents,
    and did not obey the voice of the LORD.
Therefore he raised his hand and swore to them
    that he would make them fall in the wilderness,
and would make their offspring fall among the nations,
    scattering them among the lands.

Then they yoked themselves to the Baal of Peor,
    and ate sacrifices offered to the dead;
they provoked the LORD to anger with their deeds,
    and a plague broke out among them.
Then Phinehas stood up and intervened,
    and the plague was stayed.
And that was counted to him as righteousness
    from generation to generation forever.

They angered him at the waters of Meribah,
    and it went ill with Moses on their account,
for they made his spirit bitter,
    and he spoke rashly with his lips.

They did not destroy the peoples,
    as the LORD commanded them,
but they mixed with the nations
    and learned to do as they did.
They served their idols,
    which became a snare to them.
They sacrificed their sons
    and their daughters to the demons;
they poured out innocent blood,
    the blood of their sons and daughters,
whom they sacrificed to the idols of Canaan,

and the land was polluted with blood.
Thus they became unclean by their acts,
and played the whore in their deeds.

Then the anger of the LORD was kindled against his people,
and he abhorred his heritage;
he gave them into the hand of the nations,
so that those who hated them ruled over them.
Their enemies oppressed them,
and they were brought into subjection under their power.
Many times he delivered them,
but they were rebellious in their purposes
and were brought low through their iniquity.

Nevertheless, he looked upon their distress,
when he heard their cry.
For their sake he remembered his covenant,
and relented according to the abundance of his steadfast love.
He caused them to be pitied
by all those who held them captive.

Save us, O LORD our God,
and gather us from among the nations,
that we may give thanks to your holy name
and glory in your praise.

Blessed be the LORD, the God of Israel,
from everlasting to everlasting!
And let all the people say, "Amen!"
Praise the LORD!

BOOK FIVE

PSALM 107

Give praise to God, who answers the prayers of the needy.

Oh give thanks to the LORD, for he is good,
*   for his steadfast love endures forever!*
Let the redeemed of the LORD say so,
*   whom he has redeemed from trouble*
and gathered in from the lands,
*   from the east and from the west,*
*   from the north and from the south.*

Some wandered in desert wastes,
*   finding no way to a city to dwell in;*
hungry and thirsty,
*   their soul fainted within them.*
Then they cried to the LORD in their trouble,
*   and he delivered them from their distress.*
He led them by a straight way
*   till they reached a city to dwell in.*
Let them thank the LORD for his steadfast love,
*   for his wondrous works to the children of man!*
For he satisfies the longing soul,
*   and the hungry soul he fills with good things.*

Some sat in darkness and in the shadow of death,
*   prisoners in affliction and in irons,*
for they had rebelled against the words of God,

and spurned the counsel of the Most High.
So he bowed their hearts down with hard labor;
        they fell down, with none to help.
Then they cried to the LORD in their trouble,
        and he delivered them from their distress.
He brought them out of darkness and the shadow of death,
        and burst their bonds apart.
Let them thank the LORD for his steadfast love,
        for his wondrous works to the children of man!
For he shatters the doors of bronze
        and cuts in two the bars of iron.

Some were fools through their sinful ways,
        and because of their iniquities suffered affliction;
they loathed any kind of food,
        and they drew near to the gates of death.
Then they cried to the LORD in their trouble,
        and he delivered them from their distress.
He sent out his word and healed them,
        and delivered them from their destruction.
Let them thank the LORD for his steadfast love,
        for his wondrous works to the children of man!
And let them offer sacrifices of thanksgiving,
        and tell of his deeds in songs of joy!

Some went down to the sea in ships,
        doing business on the great waters;
they saw the deeds of the LORD,
        his wondrous works in the deep.
For he commanded and raised the stormy wind,
        which lifted up the waves of the sea.
They mounted up to heaven; they went down to the depths;

    their courage melted away in their evil plight;
they reeled and staggered like drunken men
    and were at their wits' end.
Then they cried to the LORD *in their trouble,*
    and he delivered them from their distress.
He made the storm be still,
    and the waves of the sea were hushed.
Then they were glad that the waters were quiet,
    and he brought them to their desired haven.
Let them thank the LORD *for his steadfast love,*
    for his wondrous works to the children of man!
Let them extol him in the congregation of the people,
    and praise him in the assembly of the elders.

He turns rivers into a desert,
    springs of water into thirsty ground,
a fruitful land into a salty waste,
    because of the evil of its inhabitants.
He turns a desert into pools of water,
    a parched land into springs of water.
And there he lets the hungry dwell,
    and they establish a city to live in;
they sow fields and plant vineyards
    and get a fruitful yield.
By his blessing they multiply greatly,
    and he does not let their livestock diminish.

When they are diminished and brought low
    through oppression, evil, and sorrow,
he pours contempt on princes
    and makes them wander in trackless wastes;
but he raises up the needy out of affliction

and makes their families like flocks.
The upright see it and are glad,
        and all wickedness shuts its mouth.

Whoever is wise, let him attend to these things;
        let them consider the steadfast love of the Lord.

Psalm 110

A proclamation of God's favor on his chosen.

The Lord *says to my Lord:*
        "Sit at my right hand,
until I make your enemies your footstool."

The Lord *sends forth from Zion*
        your mighty scepter.
        Rule in the midst of your enemies!
Your people will offer themselves freely
        on the day of your power,
        in holy garments;
from the womb of the morning,
        the dew of your youth will be yours.
The Lord *has sworn*
        and will not change his mind,
"You are a priest forever
        after the order of Melchizedek."

The Lord is at your right hand;
        he will shatter kings on the day of his wrath.
He will execute judgment among the nations,
        filling them with corpses;
he will shatter chiefs
        over the wide earth.

He will drink from the brook by the way;
therefore he will lift up his head.

PSALM 111

An exclamation of glory to God for his power and righteousness.

Praise the LORD!
I will give thanks to the LORD with my whole heart,
in the company of the upright, in the congregation.
Great are the works of the LORD,
studied by all who delight in them.
Full of splendor and majesty is his work,
and his righteousness endures forever.
He has caused his wondrous works to be remembered;
the LORD is gracious and merciful.
He provides food for those who fear him;
he remembers his covenant forever.
He has shown his people the power of his works,
in giving them the inheritance of the nations.
The works of his hands are faithful and just;
all his precepts are trustworthy;
they are established forever and ever,
to be performed with faithfulness and uprightness.
He sent redemption to his people;
he has commanded his covenant forever.
Holy and awesome is his name!
The fear of the LORD is the beginning of wisdom;
all those who practice it have a good understanding.
His praise endures forever!

PSALM 112

Good comes to those who live in a righteous and godly manner.

Praise the LORD!
Blessed is the man who fears the LORD,
> *who greatly delights in his commandments!*
His offspring will be mighty in the land;
> *the generation of the upright will be blessed.*
Wealth and riches are in his house,
> *and his righteousness endures forever.*
Light dawns in the darkness for the upright;
> *he is gracious, merciful, and righteous.*
It is well with the man who deals generously and lends;
> *who conducts his affairs with justice.*
For the righteous will never be moved;
> *he will be remembered forever.*
He is not afraid of bad news;
> *his heart is firm, trusting in the LORD.*
His heart is steady; he will not be afraid,
> *until he looks in triumph on his adversaries.*
He has distributed freely; he has given to the poor;
> *his righteousness endures forever;*
> *his horn is exalted in honor.*
The wicked man sees it and is angry;
> *he gnashes his teeth and melts away;*
> *the desire of the wicked will perish!*

PSALM 113

God stoops down to meet the needs of the destitute.

Praise the LORD!
Praise, O servants of the LORD,
> *praise the name of the LORD!*

Blessed be the name of the LORD
from this time forth and forevermore!
From the rising of the sun to its setting,
the name of the LORD is to be praised!

The LORD is high above all nations,
and his glory above the heavens!
Who is like the LORD our God,
who is seated on high,
who looks far down
on the heavens and the earth?
He raises the poor from the dust
and lifts the needy from the ash heap,
to make them sit with princes,
with the princes of his people.
He gives the barren woman a home,
making her the joyous mother of children.
Praise the LORD!

PSALM 114

The God who delivered Israel from Egypt remains present with us and deserves our reverence.

When Israel went out from Egypt,
the house of Jacob from a people of strange language,
Judah became his sanctuary,
Israel his dominion.

The sea looked and fled;
Jordan turned back.
The mountains skipped like rams,
the hills like lambs.

What ails you, O sea, that you flee?
 O Jordan, that you turn back?
O mountains, that you skip like rams?
 O hills, like lambs?

Tremble, O earth, at the presence of the Lord,
 at the presence of the God of Jacob,
who turns the rock into a pool of water,
 the flint into a spring of water.

Psalm 116

Praise to God for salvation from death.

I love the LORD, because he has heard
 my voice and my pleas for mercy.
Because he inclined his ear to me,
 therefore I will call on him as long as I live.
The snares of death encompassed me;
 the pangs of Sheol laid hold on me;
 I suffered distress and anguish.
Then I called on the name of the LORD:
 "O LORD, I pray, deliver my soul!"

Gracious is the LORD, and righteous;
 our God is merciful.
The LORD preserves the simple;
 when I was brought low, he saved me.
Return, O my soul, to your rest;
 for the LORD has dealt bountifully with you.

For you have delivered my soul from death,
 my eyes from tears,
 my feet from stumbling;

I will walk before the LORD
    in the land of the living.

I believed, even when I spoke,
    "I am greatly afflicted";
I said in my alarm,
    "All mankind are liars."

What shall I render to the LORD
    for all his benefits to me?
I will lift up the cup of salvation
    and call on the name of the LORD,
I will pay my vows to the LORD
    in the presence of all his people.

Precious in the sight of the LORD
    is the death of his saints.
O LORD, I am your servant;
    I am your servant, the son of your maidservant.
    You have loosed my bonds.
I will offer to you the sacrifice of thanksgiving
    and call on the name of the LORD.
I will pay my vows to the LORD
    in the presence of all his people,
in the courts of the house of the LORD,
    in your midst, O Jerusalem.
Praise the LORD!

PSALM 117

A burst of praise: a short exhortation to worship God.

Praise the LORD, all nations!
    Extol him, all peoples!

For great is his steadfast love toward us,
*   and the faithfulness of the LORD endures forever.*
Praise the LORD!

PSALM 118

**Trust in God, not in people: a song of gratitude for the
redeeming works of the Lord.**

Oh give thanks to the LORD, for he is good;
*   for his steadfast love endures forever!*

Let Israel say,
*   "His steadfast love endures forever."*
Let the house of Aaron say,
*   "His steadfast love endures forever."*
Let those who fear the LORD say,
*   "His steadfast love endures forever."*

Out of my distress I called on the LORD;
*   the LORD answered me and set me free.*
The LORD is on my side; I will not fear.
*   What can man do to me?*
The LORD is on my side as my helper;
*   I shall look in triumph on those who hate me.*

It is better to take refuge in the LORD
*   than to trust in man.*
It is better to take refuge in the LORD
*   than to trust in princes.*

All nations surrounded me;
*   in the name of the LORD I cut them off!*

They surrounded me, surrounded me on every side;
    in the name of the LORD I cut them off!
They surrounded me like bees;
        they went out like a fire among thorns;
        in the name of the LORD I cut them off!
I was pushed hard, so that I was falling,
        but the LORD helped me.

The LORD is my strength and my song;
        he has become my salvation.
Glad songs of salvation
        are in the tents of the righteous:
"The right hand of the LORD does valiantly,
        the right hand of the LORD exalts,
        the right hand of the LORD does valiantly!"

I shall not die, but I shall live,
        and recount the deeds of the LORD.
The LORD has disciplined me severely,
        but he has not given me over to death.

Open to me the gates of righteousness,
        that I may enter through them
        and give thanks to the LORD.
This is the gate of the LORD;
        the righteous shall enter through it.
I thank you that you have answered me
        and have become my salvation.
The stone that the builders rejected
        has become the cornerstone.
This is the LORD's doing;
        it is marvelous in our eyes.

This is the day that the LORD has made;
    let us rejoice and be glad in it.

Save us, we pray, O LORD!
    O LORD, we pray, give us success!

Blessed is he who comes in the name of the LORD!
    We bless you from the house of the LORD.
The LORD is God,
    and he has made his light to shine upon us.
Bind the festal sacrifice with cords,
    up to the horns of the altar!

You are my God, and I will give thanks to you;
    you are my God; I will extol you.
Oh give thanks to the LORD, for he is good;
    for his steadfast love endures forever!

PSALM 119

In praise of God's word and his ways.

Aleph
Blessed are those whose way is blameless,
    who walk in the law of the LORD!
Blessed are those who keep his testimonies,
    who seek him with their whole heart,
who also do no wrong,
    but walk in his ways!
You have commanded your precepts
    to be kept diligently.
Oh that my ways may be steadfast
    in keeping your statutes!
Then I shall not be put to shame,

having my eyes fixed on all your commandments.
I will praise you with an upright heart,
    when I learn your righteous rules.
I will keep your statutes;
    do not utterly forsake me!

Beth
How can a young man keep his way pure?
    By guarding it according to your word.
With my whole heart I seek you;
    let me not wander from your commandments!
I have stored up your word in my heart,
    that I might not sin against you.
*Blessed are you, O L*ORD*;*
    teach me your statutes!
With my lips I declare
    all the rules of your mouth.
In the way of your testimonies I delight
    as much as in all riches.
I will meditate on your precepts
    and fix my eyes on your ways.
I will delight in your statutes;
    I will not forget your word.

Gimel
Deal bountifully with your servant,
    that I may live and keep your word.
Open my eyes, that I may behold
    wondrous things out of your law.
I am a sojourner on the earth;
    hide not your commandments from me!
My soul is consumed with longing

for your rules at all times.
You rebuke the insolent, accursed ones,
who wander from your commandments.
Take away from me scorn and contempt,
for I have kept your testimonies.
Even though princes sit plotting against me,
your servant will meditate on your statutes.
Your testimonies are my delight;
they are my counselors.

Daleth
My soul clings to the dust;
give me life according to your word!
When I told of my ways, you answered me;
teach me your statutes!
Make me understand the way of your precepts,
and I will meditate on your wondrous works.
My soul melts away for sorrow;
strengthen me according to your word!
Put false ways far from me
and graciously teach me your law!
I have chosen the way of faithfulness;
I set your rules before me.
I cling to your testimonies, O LORD;
let me not be put to shame!
I will run in the way of your commandments
when you enlarge my heart!

He
Teach me, O LORD, the way of your statutes;
and I will keep it to the end.
Give me understanding, that I may keep your law

and observe it with my whole heart.
Lead me in the path of your commandments,
     for I delight in it.
Incline my heart to your testimonies,
     and not to selfish gain!
Turn my eyes from looking at worthless things;
     and give me life in your ways.
Confirm to your servant your promise,
     that you may be feared.
Turn away the reproach that I dread,
     for your rules are good.
Behold, I long for your precepts;
     in your righteousness give me life!

Waw
Let your steadfast love come to me, O LORD,
     your salvation according to your promise;
then shall I have an answer for him who taunts me,
     for I trust in your word.
And take not the word of truth utterly out of my mouth,
     for my hope is in your rules.
I will keep your law continually,
     forever and ever,
and I shall walk in a wide place,
     for I have sought your precepts.
I will also speak of your testimonies before kings
     and shall not be put to shame,
for I find my delight in your commandments,
     which I love.
I will lift up my hands toward your commandments, which I love,
     and I will meditate on your statutes.

Zayin
Remember your word to your servant,
  in which you have made me hope.
This is my comfort in my affliction,
  that your promise gives me life.
The insolent utterly deride me,
  but I do not turn away from your law.
When I think of your rules from of old,
  I take comfort, O LORD.
Hot indignation seizes me because of the wicked,
  who forsake your law.
Your statutes have been my songs
  in the house of my sojourning.
I remember your name in the night, O LORD,
  and keep your law.
This blessing has fallen to me,
  that I have kept your precepts.

Heth
The LORD is my portion;
  I promise to keep your words.
I entreat your favor with all my heart;
  be gracious to me according to your promise.
When I think on my ways,
  I turn my feet to your testimonies;
I hasten and do not delay
  to keep your commandments.
Though the cords of the wicked ensnare me,
  I do not forget your law.
At midnight I rise to praise you,
  because of your righteous rules.
I am a companion of all who fear you,

of those who keep your precepts.
The earth, O LORD, is full of your steadfast love;
 teach me your statutes!

Teth
You have dealt well with your servant,
 O LORD, according to your word.
Teach me good judgment and knowledge,
 for I believe in your commandments.
Before I was afflicted I went astray,
 but now I keep your word.
You are good and do good;
 teach me your statutes.
The insolent smear me with lies,
 but with my whole heart I keep your precepts;
their heart is unfeeling like fat,
 but I delight in your law.
It is good for me that I was afflicted,
 that I might learn your statutes.
The law of your mouth is better to me
 than thousands of gold and silver pieces.

Yodh
Your hands have made and fashioned me;
 give me understanding that I may learn your commandments.
Those who fear you shall see me and rejoice,
 because I have hoped in your word.
I know, O LORD, that your rules are righteous,
 and that in faithfulness you have afflicted me.
Let your steadfast love comfort me
 according to your promise to your servant.
Let your mercy come to me, that I may live;

for your law is my delight.
Let the insolent be put to shame,
   because they have wronged me with falsehood;
as for me, I will meditate on your precepts.
   Let those who fear you turn to me,
that they may know your testimonies.
May my heart be blameless in your statutes,
   that I may not be put to shame!

Kaph
My soul longs for your salvation;
   I hope in your word.
My eyes long for your promise;
   I ask, "When will you comfort me?"
For I have become like a wineskin in the smoke,
   yet I have not forgotten your statutes.
How long must your servant endure?
   When will you judge those who persecute me?
The insolent have dug pitfalls for me;
   they do not live according to your law.
All your commandments are sure;
   they persecute me with falsehood; help me!
They have almost made an end of me on earth,
   but I have not forsaken your precepts.
In your steadfast love give me life,
   that I may keep the testimonies of your mouth.

Lamedh
Forever, O LORD, your word
   is firmly fixed in the heavens.
Your faithfulness endures to all generations;

you have established the earth, and it stands fast.
By your appointment they stand this day,
    for all things are your servants.
If your law had not been my delight,
    I would have perished in my affliction.
I will never forget your precepts,
    for by them you have given me life.
I am yours; save me,
    for I have sought your precepts.
The wicked lie in wait to destroy me,
    but I consider your testimonies.
I have seen a limit to all perfection,
    but your commandment is exceedingly broad.

Mem
Oh how I love your law!
    It is my meditation all the day.
Your commandment makes me wiser than my enemies,
    for it is ever with me.
I have more understanding than all my teachers,
    for your testimonies are my meditation.
I understand more than the aged,
    for I keep your precepts.
I hold back my feet from every evil way,
    in order to keep your word.
I do not turn aside from your rules,
    for you have taught me.
How sweet are your words to my taste,
    sweeter than honey to my mouth!
Through your precepts I get understanding;
    therefore I hate every false way.

Psalms

Nun
Your word is a lamp to my feet
*   and a light to my path.*
I have sworn an oath and confirmed it,
*   to keep your righteous rules.*
I am severely afflicted;
*   give me life, O Lord, according to your word!*
Accept my freewill offerings of praise, O Lord,
*   and teach me your rules.*
I hold my life in my hand continually,
*   but I do not forget your law.*
The wicked have laid a snare for me,
*   but I do not stray from your precepts.*
Your testimonies are my heritage forever,
*   for they are the joy of my heart.*
I incline my heart to perform your statutes
*   forever, to the end.*

Samekh
I hate the double-minded,
*   but I love your law.*
You are my hiding place and my shield;
*   I hope in your word.*
Depart from me, you evildoers,
*   that I may keep the commandments of my God.*
Uphold me according to your promise, that I may live,
*   and let me not be put to shame in my hope!*
Hold me up, that I may be safe
*   and have regard for your statutes continually!*
You spurn all who go astray from your statutes,
*   for their cunning is in vain.*
All the wicked of the earth you discard like dross,

therefore I love your testimonies.
My flesh trembles for fear of you,
and I am afraid of your judgments.

Ayin
I have done what is just and right;
do not leave me to my oppressors.
Give your servant a pledge of good;
let not the insolent oppress me.
My eyes long for your salvation
and for the fulfillment of your righteous promise.
Deal with your servant according to your steadfast love,
and teach me your statutes.
I am your servant; give me understanding,
that I may know your testimonies!
It is time for the LORD to act,
for your law has been broken.
Therefore I love your commandments
above gold, above fine gold.
Therefore I consider all your precepts to be right;
I hate every false way.

Pe
Your testimonies are wonderful;
therefore my soul keeps them.
The unfolding of your words gives light;
it imparts understanding to the simple.
I open my mouth and pant,
because I long for your commandments.
Turn to me and be gracious to me,
as is your way with those who love your name.
Keep steady my steps according to your promise,

and let no iniquity get dominion over me.
Redeem me from man's oppression,
    that I may keep your precepts.
Make your face shine upon your servant,
    and teach me your statutes.
My eyes shed streams of tears,
    because people do not keep your law.

Tsadhe
Righteous are you, O LORD,
    and right are your rules.
You have appointed your testimonies in righteousness
    and in all faithfulness.
My zeal consumes me,
    because my foes forget your words.
Your promise is well tried,
    and your servant loves it.
I am small and despised,
    yet I do not forget your precepts.
Your righteousness is righteous forever,
    and your law is true.
Trouble and anguish have found me out,
    but your commandments are my delight.
Your testimonies are righteous forever;
    give me understanding that I may live.

Qoph
With my whole heart I cry; answer me, O LORD!
    I will keep your statutes.
I call to you; save me,
    that I may observe your testimonies.

I rise before dawn and cry for help;
*   I hope in your words.*
My eyes are awake before the watches of the night,
*   that I may meditate on your promise.*
Hear my voice according to your steadfast love;
*   O LORD, according to your justice give me life.*
They draw near who persecute me with evil purpose;
*   they are far from your law.*
But you are near, O LORD,
*   and all your commandments are true.*
Long have I known from your testimonies
*   that you have founded them forever.*

Resh
Look on my affliction and deliver me,
*   for I do not forget your law.*
Plead my cause and redeem me;
*   give me life according to your promise!*
Salvation is far from the wicked,
*   for they do not seek your statutes.*
Great is your mercy, O LORD;
*   give me life according to your rules.*
Many are my persecutors and my adversaries,
*   but I do not swerve from your testimonies.*
I look at the faithless with disgust,
*   because they do not keep your commands.*
Consider how I love your precepts!
*   Give me life according to your steadfast love.*
The sum of your word is truth,
*   and every one of your righteous rules endures forever.*

Sin and Shin
Princes persecute me without cause,
    but my heart stands in awe of your words.
I rejoice at your word
    like one who finds great spoil.
I hate and abhor falsehood,
    but I love your law.
Seven times a day I praise you
    for your righteous rules.
Great peace have those who love your law;
    nothing can make them stumble.
I hope for your salvation, O LORD,
    and I do your commandments.
My soul keeps your testimonies;
    I love them exceedingly.
I keep your precepts and testimonies,
    for all my ways are before you.

Taw
Let my cry come before you, O LORD;
    give me understanding according to your word!
Let my plea come before you;
    deliver me according to your word.
My lips will pour forth praise,
    for you teach me your statutes.
My tongue will sing of your word,
    for all your commandments are right.
Let your hand be ready to help me,
    for I have chosen your precepts.
I long for your salvation, O LORD,
    and your law is my delight.
Let my soul live and praise you,

and let your rules help me.
I have gone astray like a lost sheep; seek your servant,
    for I do not forget your commandments.

PSALM 120

An individual prays for relief from the allegations of false accusers.

In my distress I called to the LORD,
    and he answered me.
Deliver me, O LORD,
    from lying lips,
    from a deceitful tongue.

What shall be given to you,
    and what more shall be done to you,
    you deceitful tongue?
A warrior's sharp arrows,
    with glowing coals of the broom tree!

Woe to me, that I sojourn in Meshech,
    that I dwell among the tents of Kedar!
Too long have I had my dwelling
    among those who hate peace.
I am for peace,
    but when I speak, they are for war!

PSALM 121

The Lord will watch over and protect you.

I lift up my eyes to the hills.
    From where does my help come?

My help comes from the LORD,
>who made heaven and earth.

He will not let your foot be moved;
>he who keeps you will not slumber.
Behold, he who keeps Israel
>will neither slumber nor sleep.

The LORD is your keeper;
>the LORD is your shade on your right hand.
The sun shall not strike you by day,
>nor the moon by night.

The LORD will keep you from all evil;
>he will keep your life.
The LORD will keep
>your going out and your coming in
>from this time forth and forevermore.

PSALM 122

A prayer lifting up Jerusalem.

I was glad when they said to me,
>"Let us go to the house of the LORD!"
Our feet have been standing
>within your gates, O Jerusalem!

Jerusalem—built as a city
>that is bound firmly together,
to which the tribes go up,
>the tribes of the LORD,

as was decreed for Israel,
>to give thanks to the name of the LORD.
There thrones for judgment were set,
>the thrones of the house of David.

Pray for the peace of Jerusalem!
>"May they be secure who love you!
Peace be within your walls
>and security within your towers!"
For my brothers and companions' sake
>I will say, "Peace be within you!"
For the sake of the house of the LORD our God,
>I will seek your good.

PSALM 123

A humble and desperate people cry out to God for mercy.

To you I lift up my eyes,
>O you who are enthroned in the heavens!
Behold, as the eyes of servants
>look to the hand of their master,
as the eyes of a maidservant
>to the hand of her mistress,
so our eyes look to the LORD our God,
>till he has mercy upon us.

Have mercy upon us, O LORD, have mercy upon us,
>for we have had more than enough of contempt.
Our soul has had more than enough
>of the scorn of those who are at ease,
>of the contempt of the proud.

PSALM 124

God is glorified for rescuing his people from their enemies.

If it had not been the LORD who was on our side—
    let Israel now say—
if it had not been the LORD who was on our side
    when people rose up against us,
then they would have swallowed us up alive,
    when their anger was kindled against us;
then the flood would have swept us away,
    the torrent would have gone over us;
then over us would have gone
    the raging waters.

Blessed be the LORD,
    who has not given us
    as prey to their teeth!
We have escaped like a bird
    from the snare of the fowlers;
the snare is broken,
    and we have escaped!

Our help is in the name of the LORD,
    who made heaven and earth.

PSALM 126

**Exultation for God's past restoration of Zion and a plea
for him to reinstate his people.**

When the LORD restored the fortunes of Zion,
    we were like those who dream.
Then our mouth was filled with laughter,
    and our tongue with shouts of joy;

then they said among the nations,
> *"The LORD has done great things for them."*
The LORD has done great things for us;
> *we are glad.*

Restore our fortunes, O LORD,
> *like streams in the Negeb!*
Those who sow in tears
> *shall reap with shouts of joy!*
He who goes out weeping,
> *bearing the seed for sowing,*
shall come home with shouts of joy,
> *bringing his sheaves with him.*

PSALM 127

Wisdom for the home: all blessing and security come from God.

Unless the LORD builds the house,
> *those who build it labor in vain.*
Unless the LORD watches over the city,
> *the watchman stays awake in vain.*
It is in vain that you rise up early
> *and go late to rest,*
eating the bread of anxious toil;
> *for he gives to his beloved sleep.*

Behold, children are a heritage from the LORD,
> *the fruit of the womb a reward.*
Like arrows in the hand of a warrior
> *are the children of one's youth.*
Blessed is the man
> *who fills his quiver with them!*

He shall not be put to shame
when he speaks with his enemies in the gate.

PSALM 128

Wisdom for the home: a godly person is blessed.

Blessed is everyone who fears the LORD,
who walks in his ways!
You shall eat the fruit of the labor of your hands;
you shall be blessed, and it shall be well with you.

Your wife will be like a fruitful vine
within your house;
your children will be like olive shoots
around your table.
Behold, thus shall the man be blessed
who fears the LORD.

The LORD bless you from Zion!
May you see the prosperity of Jerusalem
all the days of your life!
May you see your children's children!
Peace be upon Israel!

PSALM 129

Israel prays for continued deliverance from her enemies.

"Greatly have they afflicted me from my youth"—
let Israel now say—
"Greatly have they afflicted me from my youth,
yet they have not prevailed against me.
The plowers plowed upon my back;
they made long their furrows."

The LORD is righteous;
>   *he has cut the cords of the wicked.*
May all who hate Zion
>   *be put to shame and turned backward!*
Let them be like the grass on the housetops,
>   *which withers before it grows up,*
with which the reaper does not fill his hand
>   *nor the binder of sheaves his arms,*
nor do those who pass by say,
>   *"The blessing of the LORD be upon you!*
>   *We bless you in the name of the LORD!"*

PSALM 131

In all humility: confession of trust in the Lord and encouragement for others to put their faith in him.

O LORD, my heart is not lifted up;
>   *my eyes are not raised too high;*
I do not occupy myself with things
>   *too great and too marvelous for me.*
But I have calmed and quieted my soul,
>   *like a weaned child with its mother;*
>   *like a weaned child is my soul within me.*
O Israel, hope in the LORD
>   *from this time forth and forevermore.*

PSALM 132

A prayer for the house of David.

Remember, O LORD, in David's favor,
>   *all the hardships he endured,*
how he swore to the LORD
>   *and vowed to the Mighty One of Jacob,*

"I will not enter my house
        or get into my bed,
I will not give sleep to my eyes
        or slumber to my eyelids,
until I find a place for the LORD,
        a dwelling place for the Mighty One of Jacob."

Behold, we heard of it in Ephrathah;
        we found it in the fields of Jaar.
"Let us go to his dwelling place;
        let us worship at his footstool!"

Arise, O LORD, and go to your resting place,
        you and the ark of your might.
Let your priests be clothed with righteousness,
        and let your saints shout for joy.
For the sake of your servant David,
        do not turn away the face of your anointed one.

The LORD swore to David a sure oath
        from which he will not turn back:
"One of the sons of your body
        I will set on your throne.
If your sons keep my covenant
        and my testimonies that I shall teach them,
their sons also forever
        shall sit on your throne."

For the LORD has chosen Zion;
        he has desired it for his dwelling place:
"This is my resting place forever;
        here I will dwell, for I have desired it.

I will abundantly bless her provisions;
      I will satisfy her poor with bread.
Her priests I will clothe with salvation,
      and her saints will shout for joy.
There I will make a horn to sprout for David;
      I have prepared a lamp for my anointed.
His enemies I will clothe with shame,
      but on him his crown will shine."

PSALM 133

It is good for the people of God to be united.

Behold, how good and pleasant it is
      when brothers dwell in unity!
It is like the precious oil on the head,
      running down on the beard,
on the beard of Aaron,
      running down on the collar of his robes!
It is like the dew of Hermon,
      which falls on the mountains of Zion!
For there the LORD has commanded the blessing,
      life forevermore.

PSALM 134

An invitation to worship God.

Come, bless the LORD, all you servants of the LORD,
      who stand by night in the house of the LORD!
Lift up your hands to the holy place
      and bless the LORD!

May the LORD bless you from Zion,
      he who made heaven and earth!

PSALM 135

God is the Lord of all; he alone is to be glorified.

Praise the LORD!
Praise the name of the LORD,
*   give praise, O servants of the LORD,*
who stand in the house of the LORD,
*   in the courts of the house of our God!*
Praise the LORD, for the LORD is good;
*   sing to his name, for it is pleasant!*
For the LORD has chosen Jacob for himself,
*   Israel as his own possession.*

For I know that the LORD is great,
*   and that our Lord is above all gods.*
Whatever the LORD pleases, he does,
*   in heaven and on earth,*
*   in the seas and all deeps.*
He it is who makes the clouds rise at the end of the earth,
*   who makes lightnings for the rain*
*   and brings forth the wind from his storehouses.*

He it was who struck down the firstborn of Egypt,
*   both of man and of beast;*
who in your midst, O Egypt,
*   sent signs and wonders*
*   against Pharaoh and all his servants;*
who struck down many nations
*   and killed mighty kings,*
Sihon, king of the Amorites,
*   and Og, king of Bashan,*
*   and all the kingdoms of Canaan,*

and gave their land as a heritage,
     a heritage to his people Israel.

Your name, O LORD, endures forever,
     your renown, O LORD, throughout all ages.
For the LORD will vindicate his people
     and have compassion on his servants.

The idols of the nations are silver and gold,
     the work of human hands.
They have mouths, but do not speak;
     they have eyes, but do not see;
they have ears, but do not hear,
     nor is there any breath in their mouths.
Those who make them become like them,
     so do all who trust in them!

O house of Israel, bless the LORD!
     O house of Aaron, bless the LORD!
O house of Levi, bless the LORD!
     You who fear the LORD, bless the LORD!
Blessed be the LORD from Zion,
     he who dwells in Jerusalem!
Praise the LORD!

PSALM 136

Praise and gratitude to God, the infinite redeemer of Israel.

Give thanks to the LORD, for he is good,
     for his steadfast love endures forever.
Give thanks to the God of gods,
     for his steadfast love endures forever.

Give thanks to the Lord of lords,
for his steadfast love endures forever;

to him who alone does great wonders,
for his steadfast love endures forever;
to him who by understanding made the heavens,
for his steadfast love endures forever;
to him who spread out the earth above the waters,
for his steadfast love endures forever;
to him who made the great lights,
for his steadfast love endures forever;
the sun to rule over the day,
for his steadfast love endures forever;
the moon and stars to rule over the night,
for his steadfast love endures forever;

to him who struck down the firstborn of Egypt,
for his steadfast love endures forever;
and brought Israel out from among them,
for his steadfast love endures forever;
with a strong hand and an outstretched arm,
for his steadfast love endures forever;
to him who divided the Red Sea in two,
for his steadfast love endures forever;
and made Israel pass through the midst of it,
for his steadfast love endures forever;
but overthrew Pharaoh and his host in the Red Sea,
for his steadfast love endures forever;
to him who led his people through the wilderness,
for his steadfast love endures forever;

to him who struck down great kings,
>   *for his steadfast love endures forever;*
and killed mighty kings,
>   *for his steadfast love endures forever;*
Sihon, king of the Amorites,
>   *for his steadfast love endures forever;*
and Og, king of Bashan,
>   *for his steadfast love endures forever;*
and gave their land as a heritage,
>   *for his steadfast love endures forever;*
a heritage to Israel his servant,
>   *for his steadfast love endures forever.*

It is he who remembered us in our low estate,
>   *for his steadfast love endures forever;*
and rescued us from our foes,
>   *for his steadfast love endures forever;*
he who gives food to all flesh,
>   *for his steadfast love endures forever.*

Give thanks to the God of heaven,
>   *for his steadfast love endures forever.*

PSALM 137

Reflection on the agonies of captivity in a foreign land.

By the waters of Babylon,
>   *there we sat down and wept,*
>   *when we remembered Zion.*
On the willows there
>   *we hung up our lyres.*
For there our captors
>   *required of us songs,*

and our tormentors, mirth, saying,
> *"Sing us one of the songs of Zion!"*

How shall we sing the LORD's song
> *in a foreign land?*
If I forget you, O Jerusalem,
> *let my right hand forget its skill!*
Let my tongue stick to the roof of my mouth,
> *if I do not remember you,*
if I do not set Jerusalem
> *above my highest joy!*

Remember, O LORD, against the Edomites
> *the day of Jerusalem,*
how they said, "Lay it bare, lay it bare,
> *down to its foundations!"*
O daughter of Babylon, doomed to be destroyed,
> *blessed shall he be who repays you*
> *with what you have done to us!*
Blessed shall he be who takes your little ones
> *and dashes them against the rock!*

PSALM 138
God in his greatness still condescends in love to care for the meek.

I give you thanks, O LORD, with my whole heart;
> *before the gods I sing your praise;*
I bow down toward your holy temple
> *and give thanks to your name for your steadfast love*
> > *and your faithfulness,*
> *for you have exalted above all things*

your name and your word.
On the day I called, you answered me;
my strength of soul you increased.

All the kings of the earth shall give you thanks,
O LORD,
for they have heard the words of your mouth,
and they shall sing of the ways of the LORD,
for great is the glory of the LORD.
For though the LORD is high, he regards the lowly,
but the haughty he knows from afar.

Though I walk in the midst of trouble,
you preserve my life;
you stretch out your hand against the wrath of my
enemies,
and your right hand delivers me.
The LORD will fulfill his purpose for me;
your steadfast love, O LORD, endures forever.
Do not forsake the work of your hands.

PSALM 139

A prayer of personal transparency and God-awareness.

O LORD, you have searched me and known me!
You know when I sit down and when I rise up;
you discern my thoughts from afar.
You search out my path and my lying down
and are acquainted with all my ways.
Even before a word is on my tongue,
behold, O LORD, you know it altogether.
You hem me in, behind and before,

and lay your hand upon me.
Such knowledge is too wonderful for me;
>*it is high; I cannot attain it.*

Where shall I go from your Spirit?
>*Or where shall I flee from your presence?*
If I ascend to heaven, you are there!
>*If I make my bed in Sheol, you are there!*
If I take the wings of the morning
>*and dwell in the uttermost parts of the sea,*
even there your hand shall lead me,
>*and your right hand shall hold me.*
If I say, "Surely the darkness shall cover me,
>*and the light about me be night,"*
even the darkness is not dark to you;
>*the night is bright as the day,*
>*for darkness is as light with you.*

For you formed my inward parts;
>*you knitted me together in my mother's womb.*
I praise you, for I am fearfully and wonderfully made.
Wonderful are your works;
>*my soul knows it very well.*
My frame was not hidden from you,
when I was being made in secret,
>*intricately woven in the depths of the earth.*
Your eyes saw my unformed substance;
in your book were written, every one of them,
>*the days that were formed for me,*
>*when as yet there was none of them.*

How precious to me are your thoughts, O God!
> *How vast is the sum of them!*
If I would count them, they are more than the sand.
> *I awake, and I am still with you.*

Oh that you would slay the wicked, O God!
> *O men of blood, depart from me!*
They speak against you with malicious intent;
> *your enemies take your name in vain!*
Do I not hate those who hate you, O LORD?
> *And do I not loathe those who rise up against you?*
I hate them with complete hatred;
> *I count them my enemies.*

Search me, O God, and know my heart!
> *Try me and know my thoughts!*
And see if there be any grievous way in me,
> *and lead me in the way everlasting!*

PSALM 141

A prayer for personal integrity and for protection from sin.

O LORD, I call upon you; hasten to me!
> *Give ear to my voice when I call to you!*
Let my prayer be counted as incense before you,
> *and the lifting up of my hands as the evening sacrifice!*

Set a guard, O LORD, over my mouth;
> *keep watch over the door of my lips!*
Do not let my heart incline to any evil,
> *to busy myself with wicked deeds*

in company with men who work iniquity,
*   and let me not eat of their delicacies!*

Let a righteous man strike me—it is a kindness;
*   let him rebuke me—it is oil for my head;*
*   let my head not refuse it.*
Yet my prayer is continually against their evil deeds.
When their judges are thrown over the cliff,
*   then they shall hear my words, for they are pleasant.*
As when one plows and breaks up the earth,
*   so shall our bones be scattered at the mouth of Sheol.*

But my eyes are toward you, O GOD, my Lord;
*   in you I seek refuge; leave me not defenseless!*
Keep me from the trap that they have laid for me
*   and from the snares of evildoers!*
Let the wicked fall into their own nets,
*   while I pass by safely.*

PSALM 143

A plea for God's guidance and protection from enemies.

Hear my prayer, O LORD;
*   give ear to my pleas for mercy!*
*   In your faithfulness answer me, in your righteousness!*
Enter not into judgment with your servant,
*   for no one living is righteous before you.*

For the enemy has pursued my soul;
*   he has crushed my life to the ground;*
*   he has made me sit in darkness like those long dead.*

Therefore my spirit faints within me;
    my heart within me is appalled.

I remember the days of old;
        I meditate on all that you have done;
        I ponder the work of your hands.
I stretch out my hands to you;
        my soul thirsts for you like a parched land. Selah

Answer me quickly, O LORD!
        My spirit fails!
Hide not your face from me,
        lest I be like those who go down to the pit.
Let me hear in the morning of your steadfast love,
        for in you I trust.
Make me know the way I should go,
        for to you I lift up my soul.

Deliver me from my enemies, O LORD!
        I have fled to you for refuge!
Teach me to do your will,
        for you are my God!
Let your good Spirit lead me
        on level ground!

For your name's sake, O LORD, preserve my life!
        In your righteousness bring my soul out of trouble!
And in your steadfast love you will cut off my enemies,
        and you will destroy all the adversaries of my soul,
        for I am your servant.

PSALM 145
The glory of the King: an account of God's splendor.

I will extol you, my God and King,
    and bless your name forever and ever.
Every day I will bless you
    and praise your name forever and ever.
Great is the LORD, and greatly to be praised,
    and his greatness is unsearchable.

One generation shall commend your works to another,
    and shall declare your mighty acts.
On the glorious splendor of your majesty,
    and on your wondrous works, I will meditate.
They shall speak of the might of your awesome deeds,
    and I will declare your greatness.
They shall pour forth the fame of your abundant goodness
    and shall sing aloud of your righteousness.

The LORD is gracious and merciful,
    slow to anger and abounding in steadfast love.
The LORD is good to all,
    and his mercy is over all that he has made.

All your works shall give thanks to you, O LORD,
    and all your saints shall bless you!
They shall speak of the glory of your kingdom
    and tell of your power,
to make known to the children of man your mighty deeds,
    and the glorious splendor of your kingdom.
Your kingdom is an everlasting kingdom,
    and your dominion endures throughout all generations.

*[The L*ORD *is faithful in all his words*
    and kind in all his works.]
*The L*ORD *upholds all who are falling*
    and raises up all who are bowed down.
The eyes of all look to you,
    and you give them their food in due season.
You open your hand;
    you satisfy the desire of every living thing.
*The L*ORD *is righteous in all his ways*
    and kind in all his works.
*The L*ORD *is near to all who call on him,*
    to all who call on him in truth.
He fulfills the desire of those who fear him;
    he also hears their cry and saves them.
*The L*ORD *preserves all who love him,*
    but all the wicked he will destroy.

*My mouth will speak the praise of the L*ORD,
    and let all flesh bless his holy name forever and ever.

PSALM 148

An invitation for all of creation to extol the Lord.

*Praise the L*ORD!
*Praise the L*ORD *from the heavens;*
    praise him in the heights!
Praise him, all his angels;
    praise him, all his hosts!

Praise him, sun and moon,
    praise him, all you shining stars!
Praise him, you highest heavens,
    and you waters above the heavens!

Let them praise the name of the LORD!
>   For he commanded and they were created.
And he established them forever and ever;
>   he gave a decree, and it shall not pass away.

Praise the LORD from the earth,
>   you great sea creatures and all deeps,
fire and hail, snow and mist,
>   stormy wind fulfilling his word!

Mountains and all hills,
>   fruit trees and all cedars!
Beasts and all livestock,
>   creeping things and flying birds!

Kings of the earth and all peoples,
>   princes and all rulers of the earth!
Young men and maidens together,
>   old men and children!

Let them praise the name of the LORD,
>   for his name alone is exalted;
>   his majesty is above earth and heaven.
He has raised up a horn for his people,
>   praise for all his saints,
>   for the people of Israel who are near to him.
Praise the LORD!

PSALM 150

Make a joyful noise: a call for extravagant worship of God.

Praise the LORD!
Praise God in his sanctuary;

praise him in his mighty heavens!
Praise him for his mighty deeds;
praise him according to his excellent greatness!

Praise him with trumpet sound;
praise him with lute and harp!
Praise him with tambourine and dance;
praise him with strings and pipe!
Praise him with sounding cymbals;
praise him with loud clashing cymbals!
Let everything that has breath praise the LORD!
Praise the LORD!

PART TWO

Prayers

Prayers of Praise

For great is the LORD, and greatly to be praised,
and he is to be held in awe above all gods.
For all the gods of the peoples are idols,
but the LORD made the heavens.
Splendor and majesty are before him;
strength and joy are in his place.
Ascribe to the LORD, O clans of the peoples,
ascribe to the LORD glory and strength!
Ascribe to the LORD the glory due his name;
bring an offering and come before him!
Worship the LORD in the splendor of holiness;
tremble before him, all the earth;
yes, the world is established; it shall never be moved.

1 CHRONICLES 16:25–30

Stand up and bless the LORD your God from everlasting to everlasting. Blessed be your glorious name, which is exalted above all blessing and praise.

NEHEMIAH 9:5

Who has measured the Spirit of the LORD,
or what man shows him his counsel?
Whom did he consult,
and who made him understand?
Who taught him the path of justice,
and taught him knowledge,
and showed him the way of understanding?
Behold, the nations are like a drop from a bucket,
and are accounted as the dust on the scales;
behold, he takes up the coastlands like fine dust.

ISAIAH 40:13–15

Thus says the LORD:
"Heaven is my throne,
and the earth is my footstool;
what is the house that you would build for me,
and what is the place of my rest?
All these things my hand has made,
and so all these things came to be,
declares the LORD.
But this is the one to whom I will look:
he who is humble and contrite in spirit
and trembles at my word."

ISAIAH 66:1–2

Ah, Lord GOD! It is you who have made the heavens and the earth by your great power and by your outstretched arm! Nothing is too hard for you. You show steadfast love to thousands, but you repay the guilt of fathers to their children after them, O great and mighty God, whose name is the LORD of hosts, great in counsel and mighty in deed, whose eyes are open to all the ways of the children of man, rewarding each one according to his ways and according to the fruit of his deeds.

JEREMIAH 32:17–19

But the LORD is in his holy temple;
let all the earth keep silence before him.

HABAKKUK 2:20

Our Father in heaven,
hallowed be your name.
Your kingdom come,
your will be done,
on earth as it is in heaven.

MATTHEW 6:9–10

"Hosanna to the Son of David! Blessed is he who comes in the name of the Lord! Hosanna in the highest!"

MATTHEW 21:9

"Blessed be the Lord God of Israel,
for he has visited and redeemed his people
and has raised up a horn of salvation for us
in the house of his servant David,
as he spoke by the mouth of his holy prophets from of old,
that we should be saved from our enemies
and from the hand of all who hate us;
to show the mercy promised to our fathers
and to remember his holy covenant,
the oath that he swore to our father Abraham, to grant us
that we, being delivered from the hand of our enemies,
might serve him without fear,
in holiness and righteousness before him all our days."

LUKE 1:68−75

"Blessed is the King who comes in the name of the Lord! Peace in heaven and glory in the highest!"

LUKE 19:38

All things were made through him, and without him was not anything made that was made. In him was life, and the life was the light of men.

JOHN 1:3−4

Oh, the depth of the riches and wisdom and knowledge of God! How unsearchable are his judgments and how inscrutable his ways!

"For who has known the mind of the Lord,
or who has been his counselor?"
"Or who has given a gift to him
that he might be repaid?"

For from him and through him and to him are all things. To him be glory forever. Amen.

ROMANS 11:33—36

To the King of ages, immortal, invisible, the only God, be honor and glory forever and ever. Amen.

1 TIMOTHY 1:17

He who is the blessed and only Sovereign, the King of kings and Lord of lords, who alone has immortality, who dwells in unapproachable light, whom no one has ever seen or can see. To him be honor and eternal dominion. Amen.

1 TIMOTHY 6:15—16

Jesus Christ is the same yesterday and today and forever.

HEBREWS 13:8

Blessed be the God and Father of our Lord Jesus Christ! According to his great mercy, he has caused us to be born again to a living hope through the resurrection of Jesus Christ from the dead, to an inheritance that is imperishable, undefiled, and unfading, kept in heaven for you.

1 PETER 1:3—4

"Worthy is the Lamb who was slain, to receive power and wealth and wisdom and might and honor and glory and blessing!"

REVELATION 5:12

"Hallelujah!
Salvation and glory and power belong to our God,
for his judgments are true and just;
for he has judged the great prostitute
who corrupted the earth with her immorality,
and has avenged on her the blood of his servants."

REVELATION 19:1—2

PRAYERS OF THANKSGIVING

Oh give thanks to the LORD, for he is good;
for his steadfast love endures forever!

1 CHRONICLES 16:34

I will greatly rejoice in the LORD;
my soul shall exult in my God,
for he has clothed me with the garments of salvation;
he has covered me with the robe of righteousness,
as a bridegroom decks himself like a priest with a beautiful
  headdress,
and as a bride adorns herself with her jewels.

ISAIAH 61:10

Sing to the LORD;
praise the LORD!
For he has delivered the life of the needy
from the hand of evildoers.

JEREMIAH 20:13

"But for you who fear my name, the sun of righteousness shall
rise with healing in its wings. You shall go out leaping like calves
from the stall."

MALACHI 4:2

In that same hour he rejoiced in the Holy Spirit and said, "I thank you, Father, Lord of heaven and earth, that you have hidden these things from the wise and understanding and revealed them to little children; yes, Father, for such was your gracious will."

LUKE 10:21

"So also you have sorrow now, but I will see you again, and your hearts will rejoice, and no one will take your joy from you. In that day you will ask nothing of me. Truly, truly, I say to you, whatever you ask of the Father in my name, he will give it to you. Until now you have asked nothing in my name. Ask, and you will receive, that your joy may be full."

JOHN 16:22—24

"I have said these things to you, that in me you may have peace. In the world you will have tribulation. But take heart; I have overcome the world."

JOHN 16:33

More than that, we rejoice in our sufferings, knowing that suffering produces endurance, and endurance produces character, and character produces hope, and hope does not put us to shame, because God's love has been poured into our hearts through the Holy Spirit who has been given to us.

ROMANS 5:3—5

More than that, we also rejoice in God through our Lord Jesus Christ, through whom we have now received reconciliation.

ROMANS 5:11

What then shall we say to these things? If God is for us, who can be against us? He who did not spare his own Son but gave him up for us all, how will he not also with him graciously give us all things?

ROMANS 8:31–32

I give thanks to my God always for you because of the grace of God that was given you in Christ Jesus, that in every way you were enriched in him in all speech and all knowledge.

1 CORINTHIANS 1:4–5

But thanks be to God, who gives us the victory through our Lord Jesus Christ. Therefore, my beloved brothers, be steadfast, immovable, always abounding in the work of the Lord, knowing that in the Lord your labor is not in vain.

1 CORINTHIANS 15:57–58

But thanks be to God, who in Christ always leads us in triumphal procession, and through us spreads the fragrance of the knowledge of him everywhere.

2 CORINTHIANS 2:14

Thanks be to God for his inexpressible gift!

2 CORINTHIANS 9:15

But God, being rich in mercy, because of the great love with which he loved us, even when we were dead in our trespasses, made us alive together with Christ—by grace you have been saved.

EPHESIANS 2:4–5

For by grace you have been saved through faith. And this is not your own doing; it is the gift of God, not a result of works, so that no one may boast.

EPHESIANS 2:8–9

Rejoice in the Lord always; again I will say, Rejoice.

PHILIPPIANS 4:4

For the grace of God has appeared, bringing salvation for all people, training us to renounce ungodliness and worldly passions, and to live self-controlled, upright, and godly lives in the present age, waiting for our blessed hope, the appearing of the glory of our great God and Savior Jesus Christ, who gave himself for us to redeem us from all lawlessness and to purify for himself a people for his own possession who are zealous for good works.

TITUS 2:11–14

Therefore let us be grateful for receiving a kingdom that cannot be shaken, and thus let us offer to God acceptable worship, with reverence and awe, for our God is a consuming fire.

HEBREWS 12:28–29

PRAYERS OF CONFESSION

"But if you will not do so, behold, you have sinned against the LORD, and be sure your sin will find you out."

NUMBERS 32:23

*"You were unmindful of the Rock that bore you,
and you forgot the God who gave you birth."*

DEUTERONOMY 32:18

"O my God, I am ashamed and blush to lift my face to you, my God, for our iniquities have risen higher than our heads, and our guilt has mounted up to the heavens."

EZRA 9:6

The fear of the LORD is hatred of evil.
Pride and arrogance and the way of evil
and perverted speech I hate.

PROVERBS 8:13

"Woe is me! For I am lost; for I am a man of unclean lips, and I dwell in the midst of a people of unclean lips; for my eyes have seen the King, the LORD of hosts!"

ISAIAH 6:5

For thus said the Lord GOD, the Holy One of Israel,
"In returning and rest you shall be saved;
in quietness and in trust shall be your strength."

ISAIAH 30:15

For our transgressions are multiplied before you,
and our sins testify against us;
for our transgressions are with us,
and we know our iniquities:
transgressing, and denying the LORD,
and turning back from following our God,
speaking oppression and revolt,
conceiving and uttering from the heart lying words.

ISAIAH 59:12–13

Return, O Israel, to the LORD your God,
for you have stumbled because of your iniquity.
Take with you words

and return to the LORD;
say to him,
"Take away all iniquity;
accept what is good,
and we will pay with bulls
the vows of our lips."

HOSEA 14:1–2

"Yet even now," declares the LORD,
"return to me with all your heart,
with fasting, with weeping, and with mourning;
and rend your hearts and not your garments."
Return to the LORD your God,
for he is gracious and merciful,
slow to anger, and abounding in steadfast love;
and he relents over disaster.

JOEL 2:12–13

Who is a God like you, pardoning iniquity
and passing over transgression
for the remnant of his inheritance?
He does not retain his anger forever,
because he delights in steadfast love.
He will again have compassion on us;
he will tread our iniquities underfoot.
You will cast all our sins
into the depths of the sea.

MICAH 7:18–19

Then Peter came up and said to him, "Lord, how often will my brother sin against me, and I forgive him? As many as seven times?" Jesus said to him, "I do not say to you seven times, but seventy times seven."

MATTHEW 18:21–22

"For from within, out of the heart of man, come evil thoughts, sexual immorality, theft, murder, adultery, coveting, wickedness, deceit, sensuality, envy, slander, pride, foolishness. All these evil things come from within, and they defile a person."

MARK 7:21–23

"Just so, I tell you, there is joy before the angels of God over one sinner who repents."

LUKE 15:10

For if you live according to the flesh you will die, but if by the Spirit you put to death the deeds of the body, you will live. For all who are led by the Spirit of God are sons of God.

ROMANS 8:13–14

No temptation has overtaken you that is not common to man. God is faithful, and he will not let you be tempted beyond your ability, but with the temptation he will also provide the way of escape, that you may be able to endure it.

1 CORINTHIANS 10:13

But far be it from me to boast except in the cross of our Lord Jesus Christ, by which the world has been crucified to me, and I to the world.

GALATIANS 6:14

Let no one say when he is tempted, "I am being tempted by God," for God cannot be tempted with evil, and he himself tempts no one. But each person is tempted when he is lured and enticed by his own desire. Then desire when it has conceived gives birth to sin, and sin when it is fully grown brings forth death.

JAMES 1:13–15

If we say we have no sin, we deceive ourselves, and the truth is not in us. If we confess our sins, he is faithful and just to forgive us our sins and to cleanse us from all unrighteousness. If we say we have not sinned, we make him a liar, and his word is not in us.

1 JOHN 1:8–10

PRAYERS FOR OTHERS

"Go therefore and make disciples of all nations, baptizing them in the name of the Father and of the Son and of the Holy Spirit, teaching them to observe all that I have commanded you. And behold, I am with you always, to the end of the age."

MATTHEW 28:19–20

"But love your enemies, and do good, and lend, expecting nothing in return, and your reward will be great, and you will be sons of the Most High, for he is kind to the ungrateful and the evil. Be merciful, even as your Father is merciful."

LUKE 6:35–36

"Pay careful attention to yourselves and to all the flock, in which the Holy Spirit has made you overseers, to care for the church of God, which he obtained with his own blood."

ACTS 20:28

For as in one body we have many members, and the members do not all have the same function, so we, though many, are one body in Christ, and individually members one of another. Having gifts that differ according to the grace given to us, let us use them: if prophecy, in proportion to our faith.

ROMANS 12:4–6

Let every person be subject to the governing authorities. For there is no authority except from God, and those that exist have been instituted by God. Therefore whoever resists the authorities resists what God has appointed, and those who resist will incur judgment.

ROMANS 13:1–2

Pay to all what is owed to them: taxes to whom taxes are owed, revenue to whom revenue is owed, respect to whom respect is owed, honor to whom honor is owed.

ROMANS 13:7

May the God of endurance and encouragement grant you to live in such harmony with one another, in accord with Christ Jesus, that together you may with one voice glorify the God and Father of our Lord Jesus Christ.

ROMANS 15:5–6

Let no one seek his own good, but the good of his neighbor.

1 CORINTHIANS 10:24

For in one Spirit we were all baptized into one body—Jews or Greeks, slaves or free—and all were made to drink of one Spirit.

1 CORINTHIANS 12:13

That there may be no division in the body, but that the members may have the same care for one another. If one member suffers, all suffer together; if one member is honored, all rejoice together. Now you are the body of Christ and individually members of it.

1 CORINTHIANS 12:25−27

Bear one another's burdens, and so fulfill the law of Christ.

GALATIANS 6:2

So then, as we have opportunity, let us do good to everyone, and especially to those who are of the household of faith.

GALATIANS 6:10

There is one body and one Spirit—just as you were called to the one hope that belongs to your call—one Lord, one faith, one baptism, one God and Father of all, who is over all and through all and in all.

EPHESIANS 4:4−6

Do nothing from rivalry or conceit, but in humility count others more significant than yourselves. Let each of you look not only to his own interests, but also to the interests of others.

PHILIPPIANS 2:3−4

And may the Lord make you increase and abound in love for one another and for all, as we do for you.

1 THESSALONIANS 3:12

Remind them to be submissive to rulers and authorities, to be obedient, to be ready for every good work, to speak evil of no one, to avoid quarreling, to be gentle, and to show perfect courtesy toward all people.

TITUS 3:1−2

Let brotherly love continue. Do not neglect to show hospitality to strangers, for thereby some have entertained angels unawares. Remember those who are in prison, as though in prison with them, and those who are mistreated, since you also are in the body.

HEBREWS 13:1–3

Religion that is pure and undefiled before God, the Father, is this: to visit orphans and widows in their affliction, and to keep oneself unstained from the world.

JAMES 1:27

For this is the will of God, that by doing good you should put to silence the ignorance of foolish people. Live as people who are free, not using your freedom as a cover-up for evil, but living as servants of God. Honor everyone. Love the brotherhood. Fear God. Honor the emperor.

1 PETER 2:15–17

Whoever loves his brother abides in the light, and in him there is no cause for stumbling. But whoever hates his brother is in the darkness and walks in the darkness, and does not know where he is going, because the darkness has blinded his eyes.

1 JOHN 2:10–11

By this we know love, that he laid down his life for us, and we ought to lay down our lives for the brothers. But if anyone has the world's goods and sees his brother in need, yet closes his heart against him, how does God's love abide in him? Little children, let us not love in word or talk but in deed and in truth.

1 JOHN 3:16–18

Have mercy on those who doubt.

JUDE 22

PRAYERS FOR ONESELF

"The LORD our God be with us, as he was with our fathers. May he not leave us or forsake us, that he may incline our hearts to him, to walk in all his ways and to keep his commandments, his statutes, and his rules, which he commanded our fathers. Let these words of mine, with which I have pleaded before the LORD, be near to the LORD our God day and night, and may he maintain the cause of his servant and the cause of his people Israel, as each day requires, that all the peoples of the earth may know that the LORD is God; there is no other. Let your heart therefore be wholly true to the LORD our God, walking in his statutes and keeping his commandments, as at this day."

1 KINGS 8 : 5 7 — 6 1

And he said to him, "You shall love the Lord your God with all your heart and with all your soul and with all your mind. This is the great and first commandment. And a second is like it: You shall love your neighbor as yourself. On these two commandments depend all the Law and the Prophets."

MATTHEW 2 2 : 3 7 — 4 0

"And I tell you, ask, and it will be given to you; seek, and you will find; knock, and it will be opened to you. For everyone who asks receives, and the one who seeks finds, and to the one who knocks it will be opened."

LUKE 1 1 : 9 — 1 0

I appeal to you therefore, brothers, by the mercies of God, to present your bodies as a living sacrifice, holy and acceptable to God, which is your spiritual worship.

ROMANS 12:1

Or do you not know that your body is a temple of the Holy Spirit within you, whom you have from God? You are not your own, for you were bought with a price. So glorify God in your body.

1 CORINTHIANS 6:19–20

And let us not grow weary of doing good, for in due season we will reap, if we do not give up.

GALATIANS 6:9

For at one time you were darkness, but now you are light in the Lord. Walk as children of light (for the fruit of light is found in all that is good and right and true), and try to discern what is pleasing to the Lord.

EPHESIANS 5:8–10

Not that I am speaking of being in need, for I have learned in whatever situation I am to be content. I know how to be brought low, and I know how to abound. In any and every circumstance, I have learned the secret of facing plenty and hunger, abundance and need. I can do all things through him who strengthens me.

PHILIPPIANS 4:11–13

And you, who once were alienated and hostile in mind, doing evil deeds, he has now reconciled in his body of flesh by his death, in order to present you holy and blameless and above reproach before him.

COLOSSIANS 1:21–22

If with Christ you died to the elemental spirits of the world, why, as if you were still alive in the world, do you submit to regulations?

COLOSSIANS 2:20

Now may the God of peace himself sanctify you completely, and may your whole spirit and soul and body be kept blameless at the coming of our Lord Jesus Christ. He who calls you is faithful; he will surely do it.

1 THESSALONIANS 5:23–24

Have nothing to do with irreverent, silly myths. Rather train yourself for godliness; for while bodily training is of some value, godliness is of value in every way, as it holds promise for the present life and also for the life to come.

1 TIMOTHY 4:7–8

Let no one despise you for your youth, but set the believers an example in speech, in conduct, in love, in faith, in purity.

1 TIMOTHY 4:12

Therefore put away all filthiness and rampant wickedness and receive with meekness the implanted word, which is able to save your souls.

JAMES 1:21

For they disciplined us for a short time as it seemed best to them, but he disciplines us for our good, that we may share his holiness. For the moment all discipline seems painful rather than pleasant, but later it yields the peaceful fruit of righteousness to those who have been trained by it. Therefore lift your drooping hands and strengthen your weak knees, and make straight paths for your feet, so that what is lame may not be put out of joint but rather be healed.

HEBREWS 12:10–13

Be sober-minded; be watchful. Your adversary the devil prowls around like a roaring lion, seeking someone to devour. Resist him, firm in your faith, knowing that the same kinds of suffering are being experienced by your brotherhood throughout the world.

1 PETER 5:8–9

PRAYERS OF LAMENTATION

"What is man, that you make so much of him,
and that you set your heart on him,
visit him every morning
and test him every moment?"

JOB 7:17–18

"My days are swifter than a runner;
they flee away; they see no good.
They go by like skiffs of reed,
like an eagle swooping on the prey.
If I say, 'I will forget my complaint,
I will put off my sad face, and be of good cheer,'
I become afraid of all my suffering,
for I know you will not hold me innocent.
I shall be condemned;
why then do I labor in vain?
If I wash myself with snow
and cleanse my hands with lye,
yet you will plunge me into a pit,
and my own clothes will abhor me."

JOB 9:25–31

For in much wisdom is much vexation,
and he who increases knowledge increases sorrow.

ECCLESIASTES 1:18

"My anguish, my anguish! I writhe in pain!
Oh the walls of my heart!
My heart is beating wildly;
I cannot keep silent,
for I hear the sound of the trumpet,
the alarm of war.
Crash follows hard on crash;
the whole land is laid waste.
Suddenly my tents are laid waste,
my curtains in a moment.
How long must I see the standard
and hear the sound of the trumpet?"

JEREMIAH 4:19–21

Cursed be the man who brought the news to my father,
"A son is born to you,"
making him very glad.
Let that man be like the cities
that the LORD overthrew without pity;
let him hear a cry in the morning
and an alarm at noon,
because he did not kill me in the womb;
so my mother would have been my grave,
and her womb forever great.
Why did I come out from the womb
to see toil and sorrow,
and spend my days in shame?

JEREMIAH 20:15–18

"Is it nothing to you, all you who pass by?
Look and see if there is any sorrow like my sorrow,
which was brought upon me,

*which the L*ORD *inflicted*
on the day of his fierce anger.
From on high he sent fire;
into my bones he made it descend;
he spread a net for my feet;
he turned me back;
he has left me stunned, faint all the day long.
My transgressions were bound into a yoke;
by his hand they were fastened together;
they were set upon my neck;
he caused my strength to fail;
the Lord gave me into the hands of those whom I cannot withstand."

LAMENTATIONS 1:12−14

*"Look, O L*ORD*, for I am in distress;*
my stomach churns;
my heart is wrung within me,
because I have been very rebellious.
In the street the sword bereaves;
in the house it is like death."

LAMENTATIONS 1:20

What can I say for you, to what compare you,
O daughter of Jerusalem?
What can I liken to you, that I may comfort you,
O virgin daughter of Zion?
For your ruin is vast as the sea;
who can heal you?

LAMENTATIONS 2:13

He has made my teeth grind on gravel,
and made me cower in ashes;

my soul is bereft of peace;
I have forgotten what happiness is;
so I say, "My endurance has perished;
so has my hope from the LORD."
Remember my affliction and my wanderings,
the wormwood and the gall!
My soul continually remembers it
and is bowed down within me.
But this I call to mind,
and therefore I have hope:
The steadfast love of the LORD never ceases;
his mercies never come to an end;
they are new every morning;
great is your faithfulness.

LAMENTATIONS 3:16–23

And taking with him Peter and the two sons of Zebedee, he began to be sorrowful and troubled. Then he said to them, "My soul is very sorrowful, even to death; remain here, and watch with me."

MATTHEW 26:37–38

"Truly, truly, I say to you, you will weep and lament, but the world will rejoice. You will be sorrowful, but your sorrow will turn into joy. When a woman is giving birth, she has sorrow because her hour has come, but when she has delivered the baby, she no longer remembers the anguish, for joy that a human being has been born into the world. So also you have sorrow now, but I will see you again and your hearts will rejoice, and no one will take your joy from you."

JOHN 16:20–22

I am speaking the truth in Christ—I am not lying; my conscience bears me witness in the Holy Spirit—that I have great sorrow and unceasing anguish in my heart. For I could wish that I myself were accursed and cut off from Christ for the sake of my brothers, my kinsmen according to the flesh.

ROMANS 9:1–3

For godly grief produces a repentance that leads to salvation without regret, whereas worldly grief produces death. For see what earnestness this godly grief has produced in you, but also what eagerness to clear yourselves, what indignation, what fear, what longing, what zeal, what punishment! At every point you have proved yourselves innocent in the matter.

2 CORINTHIANS 7:10–11

PRAYERS OVER FEAR

"The LORD is my strength and my song, and he has become my salvation; this is my God, and I will praise him, my father's God, and I will exalt him."

EXODUS 15:2

"If you say in your heart, 'These nations are greater than I. How can I dispossess them?' you shall not be afraid of them but you shall remember what the LORD your God did to Pharaoh and to all Egypt, the great trials that your eyes saw, the signs, the wonders, the mighty hand, and the outstretched arm, by which the LORD your God brought you out. So will the LORD your God do to all the peoples of whom you are afraid."

DEUTERONOMY 7:17–19

"When you go out to war against your enemies, and see horses and chariots and an army larger than your own, you shall not be afraid of them, for the LORD your God is with you, who brought you up out of the land of Egypt."

DEUTERONOMY 20:1

"Be strong and courageous and do it. Do not be afraid and do not be dismayed, for the LORD God, even my God, is with you. He will not leave you or forsake you, until all the work for the service of the house of the LORD is finished."

1 CHRONICLES 28:20

"Both riches and honor come from you, and you rule over all. In your hand are power and might, and in your hand it is to make great and to give strength to all."

1 CHRONICLES 29:12

"Behold, God is my salvation; I will trust, and will not be afraid; for the LORD GOD is my strength and my song, and he has become my salvation."

ISAIAH 12:2

"Do not be afraid of them,
for I am with you to deliver you,
declares the LORD."

JEREMIAH 1:8

"Father, if you are willing, remove this cup from me. Nevertheless, not my will, but yours, be done."

LUKE 22:42

"Peace I leave with you; my peace I give to you. Not as the world gives do I give to you. Let not your hearts be troubled, neither let them be afraid."

JOHN 14:27

"Do not be afraid, but go on speaking and do not be silent, for I am with you, and no one will attack you to harm you, for I have many in this city who are my people."

ACTS 18:9–10

For you did not receive the spirit of slavery to fall back into fear, but you have received the Spirit of adoption as sons, by whom we cry, "Abba! Father!"

ROMANS 8:15

Finally, be strong in the Lord and in the strength of his might. Put on the whole armor of God, that you may be able to stand against the schemes of the devil. For we do not wrestle against flesh and blood, but against the rulers, against the authorities, against the cosmic powers over this present darkness, against the spiritual forces of evil in the heavenly places. Therefore take up the whole armor of God, that you may be able to withstand in the evil day, and having done all, to stand firm. Stand therefore, having fastened on the belt of truth, and having put on the breastplate of righteousness, and, as shoes for your feet, having put on the readiness given by the gospel of peace. In all circumstances take up the shield of faith, with which you can extinguish all the flaming darts of the evil one; and take the helmet of salvation, and the sword of the Spirit, which is the word of God, praying at all times in the Spirit, with all prayer and supplication.

EPHESIANS 6:10–18

May you be strengthened with all power, according to his glorious might, for all endurance and patience with joy, giving thanks to the Father, who has qualified you to share in the inheritance of the saints in light.

COLOSSIANS 1:11–12

For this reason I remind you to fan into flame the gift of God, which is in you through the laying on of my hands, for God gave us a spirit not of fear but of power and love and self-control. Therefore do not be ashamed of the testimony about our Lord, nor of me his prisoner, but share in suffering for the gospel by the power of God, who saved us and called us to a holy calling, not because of our works but because of his own purpose and grace, which he gave us in Christ Jesus before the ages began, and which now has been manifested through the appearing of our Savior Christ Jesus, who abolished death and brought life and immortality to light through the gospel, for which I was appointed a preacher and apostle and teacher, which is why I suffer as I do. But I am not ashamed, for I know whom I have believed, and I am convinced that he is able to guard until that Day what has been entrusted to me.

2 TIMOTHY 1 : 6 – 1 2

But the Lord stood by me and strengthened me, so that through me the message might be fully proclaimed and all the Gentiles might hear it. So I was rescued from the lion's mouth.

2 TIMOTHY 4 : 1 7

PRAYERS FOR HEALING

"And the LORD will take away from you all sickness, and none of the evil diseases of Egypt, which you knew, will he inflict on you."

DEUTERONOMY 7 : 1 5

"See now that I, even I, am he,
and there is no god beside me;
I kill and I make alive;
I wound and I heal;
and there is none that can deliver out of my hand."

DEUTERONOMY 3 2 : 3 9

"Thus says the LORD, the God of David your father: I have heard your prayer; I have seen your tears. Behold, I will heal you."

2 KINGS 20:5

"If my people who are called by my name humble themselves, and pray and seek my face and turn from their wicked ways, then I will hear from heaven and will forgive their sin and heal their land."

2 CHRONICLES 7:14

"For he wounds, but he binds up;
he shatters, but his hands heal."

JOB 5:18

For everything there is a season, and a time for every matter
     under heaven:
a time to be born, and a time to die;
a time to plant, and a time to pluck up what is planted;
a time to kill, and a time to heal.

ECCLESIASTES 3:1–3

And the LORD will strike Egypt, striking and healing, and they will return to the LORD, and he will listen to their pleas for mercy and heal them.

ISAIAH 19:22

Moreover, the light of the moon will be as the light of the sun, and the light of the sun will be sevenfold, as the light of seven days, in the day when the LORD binds up the brokenness of his people, and heals the wounds inflicted by his blow.

ISAIAH 30:26

O Lord, by these things men live, and in all these is the life of my
spirit. Oh restore me to health and make me live!

ISAIAH 38:16

Surely he has borne our griefs
and carried our sorrows;
yet we esteemed him stricken,
smitten by God, and afflicted.
But he was wounded for our transgressions;
he was crushed for our iniquities;
upon him was the chastisement that brought us peace,
and with his stripes we are healed.

ISAIAH 53:4-5

"I have seen his ways, but I will heal him;
I will lead him and restore comfort to him and his mourners,
creating the fruit of the lips.
Peace, peace, to the far and to the near," says the LORD,
"and I will heal him."

ISAIAH 57:18-19

"Return, O faithless sons;
I will heal your faithlessness."
"Behold, we come to you,
for you are the LORD our God."

JEREMIAH 3:22

Heal me, O LORD, and I shall be healed;
save me, and I shall be saved,
for you are my praise.

JEREMIAH 17:14

"And on the banks, on both sides of the river, there will grow all kinds of trees for food. Their leaves will not wither, nor their fruit fail, but they will bear fresh fruit every month, because the water for them flows from the sanctuary. Their fruit will be for food, and their leaves for healing."

E Z E K I E L 4 7 : 1 2

"Come, let us return to the LORD; for he has torn us, that he may heal us; he has struck us down, and he will bind us up."

H O S E A 6 : 1

"But for you who fear my name, the sun of righteousness shall rise with healing in its wings. You shall go out leaping like calves from the stall."

M A L A C H I 4 : 2

And he went throughout all Galilee, teaching in their synagogues and proclaiming the gospel of the kingdom and healing every disease and every affliction among the people. So his fame spread throughout all Syria, and they brought him all the sick, those afflicted with various diseases and pains, those oppressed by demons, epileptics, and paralytics, and he healed them.

M A T T H E W 4 : 2 3 – 2 4

While he was saying these things to them, behold, a ruler came in and knelt before him, saying, "My daughter has just died, but come and lay your hand on her, and she will live."

M A T T H E W 9 : 1 8

"Heal the sick, raise the dead, cleanse lepers, cast out demons."

M A T T H E W 1 0 : 8

"The blind receive their sight and the lame walk, lepers are cleansed and the deaf hear, and the dead are raised up, and the poor have good news preached to them."

MATTHEW 11:5

When he went ashore he saw a great crowd, and he had compassion on them and healed their sick.

MATTHEW 14:14

And great crowds came to him, bringing with them the lame, the blind, the crippled, the mute, and many others, and they put them at his feet, and he healed them, so that the crowd wondered, when they saw the mute speaking, the crippled healthy, the lame walking, and the blind seeing. And they glorified the God of Israel.

MATTHEW 15:30–31

And the blind and the lame came to him in the temple, and he healed them.

MATTHEW 21:14

And they were astonished beyond measure, saying, "He has done all things well. He even makes the deaf hear and the mute speak."

MARK 7:37

And he said to her, "Daughter, your faith has made you well; go in peace, and be healed of your disease."

MARK 5:34

"And these signs will accompany those who believe: in my name they will cast out demons; they will speak in new tongues; they will pick up serpents with their hands; and if they drink any deadly poison, it will not hurt them; they will lay their hands on the sick, and they will recover."

MARK 16:17-18

Therefore, confess your sins to one another and pray for one another, that you may be healed. The prayer of a righteous person has great power as it is working.

JAMES 5:16

He himself bore our sins in his body on the tree, that we might die to sin and live to righteousness. By his wounds you have been healed.

1 PETER 2:24

Beloved, I pray that all may go well with you and that you may be in good health, as it goes well with your soul.

3 JOHN 2

Prayers against Injustice

"The LORD makes poor and makes rich;
he brings low and he exalts.
He raises up the poor from the dust;
he lifts the needy from the ash heap
to make them sit with princes
and inherit a seat of honor.
For the pillars of the earth are the LORD's,
and on them he has set the world."

1 SAMUEL 2:7-8

"But he saves the needy from the sword of their mouth
and from the hand of the mighty.
So the poor have hope,
and injustice shuts her mouth."

      JOB 5:15–16

"When the ear heard, it called me blessed,
and when the eye saw, it approved,
because I delivered the poor who cried for help,
and the fatherless who had none to help him.
The blessing of him who was about to perish came upon me,
and I caused the widow's heart to sing for joy."

      JOB 29:11–13

Whoever oppresses a poor man insults his Maker,
but he who is generous to the needy honors him.

      PROVERBS 14:31

Whoever mocks the poor insults his Maker;
he who is glad at calamity will not go unpunished.

      PROVERBS 17:5

Whoever sings songs to a heavy heart
is like one who takes off a garment on a cold day,
and like vinegar on soda.
If your enemy is hungry, give him bread to eat,
and if he is thirsty, give him water to drink.

      PROVERBS 25:20–21

Open your mouth for the mute,
for the rights of all who are destitute.

Open your mouth, judge righteously,
defend the rights of the poor and needy.
       PROVERBS 31:8–9

Again I saw all the oppressions that are done under the sun. And behold, the tears of the oppressed, and they had no one to comfort them! On the side of their oppressors there was power, and there was no one to comfort them. And I thought the dead who are already dead more fortunate than the living who are still alive. But better than both is he who has not yet been and has not seen the evil deeds that are done under the sun.
       ECCLESIASTES 4:1–3

"Learn to do good;
seek justice,
correct oppression;
bring justice to the fatherless,
plead the widow's cause."
       ISAIAH 1:17

There shall come forth a shoot from the stump of Jesse,
and a branch from his roots shall bear fruit.
And the Spirit of the LORD *shall rest upon him,*
the Spirit of wisdom and understanding,
the Spirit of counsel and might,
the Spirit of knowledge and the fear of the LORD.
And his delight shall be in the fear of the LORD.
He shall not judge by what his eyes see,
or decide disputes by what his ears hear,
but with righteousness he shall judge the poor,
and decide with equity for the meek of the earth;

and he shall strike the earth with the rod of his mouth,
and with the breath of his lips he shall kill the wicked.
ISAIAH 11:1—4

He who walks righteously and speaks uprightly,
who despises the gain of oppressions,
who shakes his hands, lest they hold a bribe,
who stops his ears from hearing of bloodshed
and shuts his eyes from looking on evil,
he will dwell on the heights;
his place of defense will be the fortresses of rocks;
his bread will be given him; his water will be sure.
ISAIAH 33:15—16

"Is not this the fast that I choose:
to loose the bonds of wickedness,
to undo the straps of the yoke,
to let the oppressed go free,
and to break every yoke?
Is it not to share your bread with the hungry
and bring the homeless poor into your house;
when you see the naked, to cover him,
and not to hide yourself from your own flesh?
Then shall your light break forth like the dawn,
and your healing shall spring up speedily;
your righteousness shall go before you;
the glory of the LORD shall be your rear guard.
Then you shall call, and the LORD will answer;
you shall cry, and he will say, 'Here I am.'
If you take away the yoke from your midst,
the pointing of the finger, and speaking wickedness,
if you pour yourself out for the hungry

and satisfy the desire of the afflicted,
then shall your light rise in the darkness
and your gloom be as the noonday."

ISAIAH 58:6–10

"Thus says the LORD of hosts, Render true judgments, show kindness and mercy to one another, do not oppress the widow, the fatherless, the sojourner, or the poor, and let none of you devise evil against another in your heart."

ZECHARIAH 7:9–10

"With what shall I come before the LORD,
and bow myself before God on high?
Shall I come before him with burnt offerings,
with calves a year old?
Will the LORD be pleased with thousands of rams,
with ten thousands of rivers of oil?
Shall I give my firstborn for my transgression,
the fruit of my body for the sin of my soul?"
He has told you, O man, what is good;
and what does the LORD require of you
but to do justice, and to love kindness,
and to walk humbly with your God?

MICAH 6:6–8

"But when you give to the needy, do not let your left hand know what your right hand is doing, so that your giving may be in secret. And your Father who sees in secret will reward you."

MATTHEW 6:3–4

"'For I was hungry and you gave me food, I was thirsty and you gave me drink, I was a stranger and you welcomed me, I was naked and you clothed me, I was sick and you visited me, I was in prison and you came to me.' Then the righteous will answer him, saying, 'Lord, when did we see you hungry and feed you, or thirsty and give you drink? And when did we see you a stranger and welcome you, or naked and clothe you? And when did we see you sick or in prison and visit you?' And the King will answer them, 'Truly, I say to you, as you did it to one of the least of these my brothers, you did it to me.'"

MATTHEW 25:35–40

"If anyone would be first, he must be last of all and servant of all."

MARK 9:35

"Sell your possessions, and give to the needy. Provide yourselves with moneybags that do not grow old, with a treasure in the heavens that does not fail, where no thief approaches and no moth destroys."

LUKE 12:33

Bless those who persecute you; bless and do not curse them. Rejoice with those who rejoice, weep with those who weep. Live in harmony with one another. Do not be haughty, but associate with the lowly. Never be wise in your own sight. Repay no one evil for evil, but give thought to do what is honorable in the sight of all. If possible, so far as it depends on you, live peaceably with all. Beloved, never avenge yourselves, but leave it to the wrath of God, for it is written, "Vengeance is mine, I will repay, says the Lord." To the contrary, "if your enemy is hungry, feed him; if he is thirsty, give him something to drink; for by so doing you will heap burning coals on his head." Do not be overcome by evil, but overcome evil with good.

ROMANS 12:14–21

Listen, my beloved brothers, has not God chosen those who are
poor in the world to be rich in faith and heirs of the kingdom,
which he has promised to those who love him?

> JAMES 2:5

PRAYERS FOR PROTECTION

And he blessed Joseph and said,

"The God before whom my fathers Abraham and Isaac walked,
the God who has been my shepherd all my life long to this day,
the angel who has redeemed me from all evil, bless the boys;
and in them let my name be carried on, and the name of my
*   fathers Abraham and Isaac;*
and let them grow into a multitude in the midst of the earth."

> GENESIS 48:15–16

"The beloved of the LORD dwells in safety.
The High God surrounds him all day long,
and dwells between his shoulders."

> DEUTERONOMY 33:12

"The LORD is my rock and my fortress and my deliverer,
my God, my rock, in whom I take refuge,
my shield, and the horn of my salvation,
my stronghold and my refuge,
my savior; you save me from violence.
I call upon the LORD, who is worthy to be praised,
and I am saved from my enemies."

> 2 SAMUEL 22:2–4

"For by you I can run against a troop,
and by my God I can leap over a wall.

This God—his way is perfect;
the word of the LORD proves true;
he is a shield for all those who take refuge in him.
For who is God, but the LORD?
And who is a rock, except our God?
This God is my strong refuge
and has made my way blameless.
He made my feet like the feet of a deer
and set me secure on the heights.
He trains my hands for war,
so that my arms can bend a bow of bronze.
You have given me the shield of your salvation,
and your gentleness made me great."

    2 SAMUEL 22:30−36

"For we are slaves. Yet our God has not forsaken us in our slavery, but has extended to us his steadfast love before the kings of Persia, to grant us some reviving to set up the house of our God, to repair its ruins, and to give us protection in Judea and Jerusalem."

    EZRA 9:9

In the fear of the LORD one has strong confidence,
and his children will have a refuge.

    PROVERBS 14:26

The name of the LORD is a strong tower;
the righteous man runs into it and is safe.

    PROVERBS 18:10

The fear of man lays a snare,
but whoever trusts in the LORD is safe.

    PROVERBS 29:25

"Like birds hovering, so the LORD of hosts
will protect Jerusalem;
he will protect and deliver it;
he will spare and rescue it."
ISAIAH 31:5

Like a swallow or a crane I chirp;
I moan like a dove.
My eyes are weary with looking upward.
O Lord, I am oppressed; be my pledge of safety!
ISAIAH 38:14

For you shall not go out in haste,
and you shall not go in flight,
for the LORD will go before you,
and the God of Israel will be your rear guard.
ISAIAH 52:12

O LORD, my strength and my stronghold,
my refuge in the day of trouble.
JEREMIAH 16:19

Be not a terror to me;
you are my refuge in the day of disaster.
JEREMIAH 17:17

The Lord will rescue me from every evil deed and bring me safely into his heavenly kingdom. To him be the glory forever and ever. Amen.
2 TIMOTHY 4:18

Now may the God of peace who brought again from the dead our Lord Jesus, the great shepherd of the sheep, by the blood of the eternal covenant, equip you with everything good that you may do his will, working in us that which is pleasing in his sight, through Jesus Christ, to whom be glory forever and ever. Amen.

HEBREWS 13:20–21

Blessed be the God and Father of our Lord Jesus Christ! According to his great mercy, he has caused us to be born again to a living hope through the resurrection of Jesus Christ from the dead, to an inheritance that is imperishable, undefiled, and unfading, kept in heaven for you, who by God's power are being guarded through faith for a salvation ready to be revealed in the last time.

1 PETER 1:3–5

We know that everyone who has been born of God does not keep on sinning, but he who was born of God protects him, and the evil one does not touch him.

1 JOHN 5:18

PRAYERS FOR THE FUTURE

Then King David went in and sat before the LORD and said, "Who am I, O LORD God, and what is my house, that you have brought me thus far? And this was a small thing in your eyes, O God. You have also spoken of your servant's house for a great while to come, and have shown me future generations, O LORD God!"

1 CHRONICLES 17:16–17

The hope of the righteous brings joy,
but the expectation of the wicked will perish.

PROVERBS 10:28

Surely there is a future,
and your hope will not be cut off.

PROVERBS 23:18

But he who is joined with all the living has hope, for a living dog is
*   better than a dead lion.*
             ECCLESIASTES 9:4

I will wait for the LORD, who is hiding his face from the house of
Jacob, and I will hope in him.
             ISAIAH 8:17

Arise, shine, for your light has come,
and the glory of the LORD has risen upon you.
For behold, darkness shall cover the earth,
and thick darkness the peoples;
but the LORD will arise upon you,
and his glory will be seen upon you.
And nations shall come to your light,
and kings to the brightness of your rising.
             ISAIAH 60:1–3

"O you hope of Israel,
its savior in time of trouble,
why should you be like a stranger in the land,
like a traveler who turns aside to tarry for a night?
Why should you be like a man confused,
like a mighty warrior who cannot save?
Yet you, O LORD, are in the midst of us,
and we are called by your name;
do not leave us."
             JEREMIAH 14:8–9

"For thus says the LORD: When seventy years are completed for
Babylon, I will visit you, and I will fulfill to you my promise and
bring you back to this place. For I know the plans I have for you,
declares the LORD, plans for welfare and not for evil, to give you

a future and a hope. Then you will call upon me and come and
pray to me, and I will hear you."
JEREMIAH 29:10–12

Thus says the LORD:
"Keep your voice from weeping,
and your eyes from tears,
for there is a reward for your work,
declares the LORD,
and they shall come back from the land of the enemy.
There is hope for your future,
declares the LORD,
and your children shall come back to their own country."
JEREMIAH 31:16–17

"The LORD is my portion," says my soul,
"therefore I will hope in him."
The LORD is good to those who wait for him,
to the soul who seeks him.
It is good that one should wait quietly
for the salvation of the LORD.
It is good for a man that he bear
the yoke in his youth.
Let him sit alone in silence
when it is laid on him;
let him put his mouth in the dust—
there may yet be hope;
let him give his cheek to the one who strikes,
and let him be filled with insults.
For the Lord will not
cast off forever,
but, though he cause grief, he will have compassion

according to the abundance of his steadfast love;
for he does not willingly afflict
or grieve the children of men.
            LAMENTATIONS 3:24—33

"Behold, my servant whom I have chosen,
my beloved with whom my soul is well pleased.
I will put my Spirit upon him,
and he will proclaim justice to the Gentiles.
He will not quarrel or cry aloud,
nor will anyone hear his voice in the streets;
a bruised reed he will not break,
and a smoldering wick he will not quench,
until he brings justice to victory;
and in his name the Gentiles will hope."
            MATTHEW 12:18—21

"Therefore my heart was glad, and my tongue rejoiced;
my flesh also will dwell in hope.
For you will not abandon my soul to Hades,
or let your Holy One see corruption."
            ACTS 2:26—27

"The God who made the world and everything in it, being Lord of heaven and earth, does not live in temples made by man, nor is he served by human hands, as though he needed anything, since he himself gives to all mankind life and breath and everything. And he made from one man every nation of mankind to live on all the face of the earth, having determined allotted periods and the boundaries of their dwelling place, that they should seek God, in the hope that they might feel their way toward him and find him. Yet he is actually not far from each one of us, for 'In him we live and move and have our being'; as even some of your own poets have said, 'For we are indeed his offspring.'"

ACTS 17:24–28

"But this I confess to you, that according to the Way, which they call a sect, I worship the God of our fathers, believing everything laid down by the Law and written in the Prophets, having a hope in God, which these men themselves accept, that there will be a resurrection of both the just and the unjust. So I always take pains to have a clear conscience toward both God and man."

ACTS 24:14–16

Through him we have also obtained access by faith into this grace in which we stand, and we rejoice in hope of the glory of God. More than that, we rejoice in our sufferings, knowing that suffering produces endurance, and endurance produces character, and character produces hope, and hope does not put us to shame, because God's love has been poured into our hearts through the Holy Spirit who has been given to us.

ROMANS 5:2–5

Rejoice in hope, be patient in tribulation, be constant in prayer.

ROMANS 12:12

Indeed, we felt that we had received the sentence of death. But that was to make us rely not on ourselves but on God who raises the dead. He delivered us from such a deadly peril, and he will deliver us. On him we have set our hope that he will deliver us again.

2 CORINTHIANS 1:9–10

For I consider that the sufferings of this present time are not worth comparing with the glory that is to be revealed to us.

ROMANS 8:18

They are to do good, to be rich in good works, to be generous and ready to share, thus storing up treasure for themselves as a good foundation for the future, so that they may take hold of that which is truly life.

1 TIMOTHY 6:18—19

For the grace of God has appeared, bringing salvation for all people, training us to renounce ungodliness and worldly passions, and to live self-controlled, upright, and godly lives in the present age, waiting for our blessed hope, the appearing of the glory of our great God and Savior Jesus Christ, who gave himself for us to redeem us from all lawlessness and to purify for himself a people for his own possession who are zealous for good works.

TITUS 2:11—14

PRAYERS OF WISDOM

"Give your servant therefore an understanding mind to govern your people, that I may discern between good and evil, for who is able to govern this your great people?"

1 KINGS 3:9

"O LORD God, let your word to David my father be now fulfilled, for you have made me king over a people as numerous as the dust of the earth. Give me now wisdom and knowledge to go out and come in before this people, for who can govern this people of yours, which is so great?"

2 CHRONICLES 1:9—10

"With God are wisdom and might;
he has counsel and understanding.
If he tears down, none can rebuild;
if he shuts a man in, none can open."

   J O B   1 2 : 1 3 — 1 4

The fear of the LORD is the beginning of knowledge;
fools despise wisdom and instruction.

   P R O V E R B S   1 : 7

My son, if you receive my words
and treasure up my commandments with you,
making your ear attentive to wisdom
and inclining your heart to understanding;
yes, if you call out for insight
and raise your voice for understanding,
if you seek it like silver
and search for it as for hidden treasures,
then you will understand the fear of the LORD
and find the knowledge of God.
For the LORD gives wisdom;
from his mouth come knowledge and understanding;
he stores up sound wisdom for the upright;
he is a shield to those who walk in integrity,
guarding the paths of justice
and watching over the way of his saints.
Then you will understand righteousness and justice
and equity, every good path;
for wisdom will come into your heart,
and knowledge will be pleasant to your soul;
discretion will watch over you,
understanding will guard you,

delivering you from the way of evil,
from men of perverted speech,
who forsake the paths of uprightness
to walk in the ways of darkness,
who rejoice in doing evil
and delight in the perverseness of evil,
men whose paths are crooked,
and who are devious in their ways.

PROVERBS 2:1–15

Know that wisdom is such [sweet] to your soul;
if you find it, there will be a future,
and your hope will not be cut off.

PROVERBS 24:14

Then I saw that there is more gain in wisdom than in folly, as there is more gain in light than in darkness.

ECCLESIASTES 2:13

Who is like the wise?
And who knows the interpretation of a thing?
A man's wisdom makes his face shine,
and the hardness of his face is changed.

ECCLESIASTES 8:1

Thus says the LORD: "Let not the wise man boast in his wisdom, let not the mighty man boast in his might, let not the rich man boast in his riches, but let him who boasts boast in this, that he understands and knows me, that I am the LORD who practices steadfast love, justice, and righteousness in the earth. For in these things I delight, declares the LORD."

JEREMIAH 9:23–24

"Blessed be the name of God forever and ever,
to whom belong wisdom and might.
He changes times and seasons;
he removes kings and sets up kings;
he gives wisdom to the wise
and knowledge to those who have understanding;
he reveals deep and hidden things;
he knows what is in the darkness,
and the light dwells with him.
To you, O God of my fathers,
I give thanks and praise,
for you have given me wisdom and might,
and have now made known to me what we asked of you,
for you have made known to us the king's matter."

DANIEL 2:20–23

Oh, the depth of the riches and wisdom and knowledge of God! How unsearchable are his judgments and how inscrutable his ways!

ROMANS 11:33

For the word of the cross is folly to those who are perishing, but to us who are being saved it is the power of God. For it is written, "I will destroy the wisdom of the wise, and the discernment of the discerning I will thwart." Where is the one who is wise? Where is the scribe? Where is the debater of this age? Has not God made foolish the wisdom of the world? For since, in the wisdom of God, the world did not know God through wisdom, it pleased God through the folly of what we preach to save those who believe. For Jews demand signs and Greeks seek wisdom, but we preach Christ crucified, a stumbling block to Jews and folly to Gentiles, but to those who are called, both Jews and Greeks, Christ the power of God and the wisdom of God. For the foolishness of God is wiser than men, and the weakness of God is stronger than men.

1 CORINTHIANS 1:18−25

These things God has revealed to us through the Spirit. For the Spirit searches everything, even the depths of God. For who knows a person's thoughts except the spirit of that person, which is in him? So also no one comprehends the thoughts of God except the Spirit of God. Now we have received not the spirit of the world, but the Spirit who is from God, that we might understand the things freely given us by God. And we impart this in words not taught by human wisdom but taught by the Spirit, interpreting spiritual truths to those who are spiritual.

1 CORINTHIANS 2:10−13

In him we have redemption through his blood, the forgiveness of our trespasses, according to the riches of his grace, which he lavished upon us, in all wisdom and insight making known to us the mystery of his will, according to his purpose, which he set forth in Christ as a plan for the fullness of time, to unite all things in him, things in heaven and things on earth.

EPHESIANS 1:7−10

And so, from the day we heard, we have not ceased to pray for you, asking that you may be filled with the knowledge of his will in all spiritual wisdom and understanding, so as to walk in a manner worthy of the Lord, fully pleasing to him, bearing fruit in every good work and increasing in the knowledge of God.

COLOSSIANS 1:9−10

If any of you lacks wisdom, let him ask God, who gives generously to all without reproach, and it will be given him.

JAMES 1:5

Who is wise and understanding among you? By his good conduct let him show his works in the meekness of wisdom. But if you have bitter jealousy and selfish ambition in your hearts, do not boast and be false to the truth. This is not the wisdom that comes down from above, but is earthly, unspiritual, demonic. For where jealousy and selfish ambition exist, there will be disorder and every vile practice. But the wisdom from above is first pure, then peaceable, gentle, open to reason, full of mercy and good fruits, impartial and sincere.

JAMES 3:13–17

PRAYERS OF FAITH

Israel saw the great power that the LORD used against the Egyptians, so the people feared the LORD, and they believed in the LORD and in his servant Moses.

EXODUS 14:31

"For you, O LORD of hosts, the God of Israel, have made this revelation to your servant, saying, 'I will build you a house.' Therefore your servant has found courage to pray this prayer to you. And now, O Lord GOD, you are God, and your words are true, and you have promised this good thing to your servant. Now therefore may it please you to bless the house of your servant, so that it may continue forever before you. For you, O Lord GOD, have spoken, and with your blessing shall the house of your servant be blessed forever.

2 SAMUEL 7:27–29

Trust in the LORD with all your heart,
and do not lean on your own understanding.
In all your ways acknowledge him,
and he will make straight your paths.

PROVERBS 3:5–6

"But if God so clothes the grass of the field, which today is alive and tomorrow is thrown into the oven, will he not much more clothe you, O you of little faith?"

MATTHEW 6:30

"Lord, my servant is lying paralyzed at home, suffering terribly." And he said to him, "I will come and heal him." But the centurion replied, "Lord, I am not worthy to have you come under my roof, but only say the word, and my servant will be healed. For I too am a man under authority, with soldiers under me. And I say to one, 'Go,' and he goes, and to another, 'Come,' and he comes, and to my servant, 'Do this,' and he does it." When Jesus heard this, he marveled and said to those who followed him, "Truly, I tell you, with no one in Israel have I found such faith."

MATTHEW 8:6–10

And behold, some people brought to him a paralytic, lying on a bed. And when Jesus saw their faith, he said to the paralytic, "Take heart, my son; your sins are forgiven."

MATTHEW 9:2

Then he touched their eyes, saying, "According to your faith be it done to you."

MATTHEW 9:29

And behold, a Canaanite woman from that region came out and was crying, "Have mercy on me, O Lord, Son of David; my daughter is severely oppressed by a demon." But he did not answer her a word. And his disciples came and begged him, saying, "Send her away, for she is crying out after us." He answered, "I was sent only to the lost sheep of the house of Israel." But she came and knelt before him, saying, "Lord, help me." And he answered, "It is not right to take the children's bread and throw it to the dogs." She said, "Yes, Lord, yet even the dogs eat the crumbs that fall from their masters' table." Then Jesus answered her, "O woman, great is your faith! Be it done for you as you desire." And her daughter was healed instantly.

MATTHEW 15:22–28

"Truly, I say to you, whoever says to this mountain, 'Be taken up and thrown into the sea,' and does not doubt in his heart, but believes that what he says will come to pass, it will be done for him."

MARK 11:23

And they went and woke him, saying, "Master, Master, we are perishing!" And he awoke and rebuked the wind and the raging waves, and they ceased, and there was a calm. He said to them, "Where is your faith?" And they were afraid, and they marveled, saying to one another, "Who then is this, that he commands even winds and water, and they obey him?"

LUKE 8:24–25

"But if God so clothes the grass, which is alive in the field today, and tomorrow is thrown into the oven, how much more will he clothe you, O you of little faith!"

LUKE 12:28

The apostles said to the Lord, "Increase our faith!" And the Lord said, "If you had faith like a grain of mustard seed, you could say to this mulberry tree, 'Be uprooted and planted in the sea,' and it would obey you."

LUKE 17:5–6

Now at Lystra there was a man sitting who could not use his feet. He was crippled from birth and had never walked. He listened to Paul speaking. And Paul, looking intently at him and seeing that he had faith to be made well, said in a loud voice, "Stand upright on your feet." And he sprang up and began walking.

ACTS 14:8–10

For I long to see you, that I may impart to you some spiritual gift to strengthen you—that is, that we may be mutually encouraged by each other's faith, both yours and mine.

ROMANS 1:11–12

Now faith is the assurance of things hoped for, the conviction of things not seen.

HEBREWS 11:1

But let him ask in faith, with no doubting, for the one who doubts is like a wave of the sea that is driven and tossed by the wind.

JAMES 1:6

PRAYERS OF BLESSING

"And I will make of you a great nation, and I will bless you and make your name great, so that you will be a blessing."

GENESIS 12:2

And Moses and Aaron went into the tent of meeting, and when they came out they blessed the people, and the glory of the LORD appeared to all the people.

LEVITICUS 9:23

"The LORD bless you and keep you;
the LORD make his face to shine upon you and be gracious to you;
the LORD lift up his countenance upon you and give you peace."

NUMBERS 6:24–26

"May the LORD, the God of your fathers, make you a thousand times as many as you are and bless you, as he has promised you!"
DEUTERONOMY 1:11

"The eternal God is your dwelling place, and underneath are the everlasting arms.
And he thrust out the enemy before you and said, Destroy.
So Israel lived in safety, Jacob lived alone,
in a land of grain and wine, whose heavens drop down dew.
Happy are you, O Israel! Who is like you, a people saved by the LORD,
the shield of your help, and the sword of your triumph!
Your enemies shall come fawning to you, and you shall tread upon their backs."
DEUTERONOMY 33:27–29

"Give, and it will be given to you. Good measure, pressed down, shaken together, running over, will be put into your lap. For with the measure you use it will be measured back to you."
LUKE 6:38

"Peace be to this house!"
LUKE 10:5

"Peace to you!"
LUKE 24:36

May the God of peace be with you all. Amen.
ROMANS 15:33

Grace to you and peace from God our Father and the Lord Jesus Christ.
1 CORINTHIANS 1:3

The grace of our Lord Jesus Christ be with your spirit, brothers. Amen.

GALATIANS 6:18

Grace to you and peace from God our Father and the Lord Jesus Christ. Blessed be the God and Father of our Lord Jesus Christ, who has blessed us in Christ with every spiritual blessing in the heavenly places, even as he chose us in him before the foundation of the world, that we should be holy and blameless before him. In love he predestined us for adoption as sons through Jesus Christ, according to the purpose of his will, to the praise of his glorious grace, with which he has blessed us in the Beloved.

EPHESIANS 1:2—6

For this reason I bow my knees before the Father, from whom every family in heaven and on earth is named, that according to the riches of his glory he may grant you to be strengthened with power through his Spirit in your inner being, so that Christ may dwell in your hearts through faith—that you, being rooted and grounded in love, may have strength to comprehend with all the saints what is the breadth and length and height and depth, and to know the love of Christ that surpasses knowledge, that you may be filled with all the fullness of God.

EPHESIANS 3:14—19

To this end we always pray for you, that our God may make you worthy of his calling and may fulfill every resolve for good and every work of faith by his power, so that the name of our Lord Jesus may be glorified in you, and you in him, according to the grace of our God and the Lord Jesus Christ.

2 THESSALONIANS 1:11—12

Now may the Lord of peace himself give you peace at all times in every way. The Lord be with you all.

2 THESSALONIANS 3:16

Blessed is the man who remains steadfast under trial, for when he has stood the test he will receive the crown of life, which God has promised to those who love him.

JAMES 1:12

PRAYERS OF LEADERS AND FOR LEADERS

"So I lay prostrate before the LORD for these forty days and forty nights, because the LORD had said he would destroy you. And I prayed to the LORD, 'O Lord GOD, do not destroy your people and your heritage, whom you have redeemed through your greatness, whom you have brought out of Egypt with a mighty hand. Remember your servants, Abraham, Isaac, and Jacob. Do not regard the stubbornness of this people, or their wickedness or their sin, lest the land from which you brought us say, 'Because the LORD was not able to bring them into the land that he promised them, and because he hated them, he has brought them out to put them to death in the wilderness.' For they are your people and your heritage, whom you brought out by your great power and by your outstretched arm."

DEUTERONOMY 9:25–29

"Be strong and courageous, for you shall go with this people into the land that the LORD has sworn to their fathers to give them, and you shall put them in possession of it."

DEUTERONOMY 31:7

And the LORD turned to him and said, "Go in this might of yours and save Israel from the hand of Midian; do not I send you?"

JUDGES 6:14

Then Gideon said to God, "If you will save Israel by my hand, as you have said, behold, I am laying a fleece of wool on the threshing floor. If there is dew on the fleece alone, and it is dry on all the ground, then I shall know that you will save Israel by my hand, as you have said." And it was so. When he rose early next morning and squeezed the fleece, he wrung enough dew from the fleece to fill a bowl with water. Then Gideon said to God, "Let not your anger burn against me; let me speak just once more. Please let me test just once more with the fleece. Please let it be dry on the fleece only, and on all the ground let there be dew." And God did so that night; and it was dry on the fleece only, and on all the ground there was dew.

JUDGES 6:36–40

"The greatest among you shall be your servant. Whoever exalts himself will be humbled, and whoever humbles himself will be exalted."

MATTHEW 23:11–12

So we do not lose heart. Though our outer self is wasting away, our inner self is being renewed day by day. For this light momentary affliction is preparing for us an eternal weight of glory beyond all comparison, as we look not to the things that are seen but to the things that are unseen. For the things that are seen are transient, but the things that are unseen are eternal.

2 CORINTHIANS 4:16–18

And it is my prayer that your love may abound more and more, with knowledge and all discernment, so that you may approve what is excellent, and so be pure and blameless for the day of Christ, filled with the fruit of righteousness that comes through Jesus Christ, to the glory and praise of God.

PHILIPPIANS 1:9–11

We have not ceased to pray for you, asking that you may be filled with the knowledge of his will in all spiritual wisdom and understanding, so as to walk in a manner worthy of the Lord, fully pleasing to him, bearing fruit in every good work and increasing in the knowledge of God.

COLOSSIANS 1:9–10

To this end we always pray for you, that our God may make you worthy of his calling and may fulfill every resolve for good and every work of faith by his power, so that the name of our Lord Jesus may be glorified in you, and you in him, according to the grace of our God and the Lord Jesus Christ.

2 THESSALONIANS 1:11–12

And we desire each one of you to show the same earnestness to have the full assurance of hope until the end, so that you may not be sluggish, but imitators of those who through faith and patience inherit the promises.

HEBREWS 6:11–12

Therefore, since we are surrounded by so great a cloud of witnesses, let us also lay aside every weight, and sin which clings so closely, and let us run with endurance the race that is set before us, looking to Jesus, the founder and perfecter of our faith, who for the joy that was set before him endured the cross, despising the shame, and is seated at the right hand of the throne of God.

Consider him who endured from sinners such hostility against himself, so that you may not grow weary or fainthearted.

HEBREWS 12:1–3

Let every person be quick to hear, slow to speak, slow to anger; for the anger of man does not produce the righteousness of God. Therefore put away all filthiness and rampant wickedness and receive with meekness the implanted word, which is able to save your souls. But be doers of the word, and not hearers only, deceiving yourselves. For if anyone is a hearer of the word and not a doer, he is like a man who looks intently at his natural face in a mirror. For he looks at himself and goes away and at once forgets what he was like. But the one who looks into the perfect law, the law of liberty, and perseveres, being no hearer who forgets but a doer who acts, he will be blessed in his doing.

JAMES 1:19–25

PRAYERS FOR THE CHURCH

So the church throughout all Judea and Galilee and Samaria had peace and was being built up. And walking in the fear of the Lord and in the comfort of the Holy Spirit, it multiplied.

ACTS 9:31

And when they had appointed elders for them in every church, with prayer and fasting they committed them to the Lord in whom they had believed.

ACTS 14:23

So the churches were strengthened in the faith, and they increased in numbers daily.

ACTS 16:5

I appeal to you, brothers, by the name of our Lord Jesus Christ, that all of you agree, and that there be no divisions among you, but that you be united in the same mind and the same judgment.

1 CORINTHIANS 1:10

Now there are varieties of gifts, but the same Spirit; and there are varieties of service, but the same Lord; and there are varieties of activities, but it is the same God who empowers them all in everyone. To each is given the manifestation of the Spirit for the common good. For to one is given through the Spirit the utterance of wisdom, and to another the utterance of knowledge according to the same Spirit, to another faith by the same Spirit, to another gifts of healing by the one Spirit, to another the working of miracles, to another prophecy, to another the ability to distinguish between spirits, to another various kinds of tongues, to another the interpretation of tongues. All these are empowered by one and the same Spirit, who apportions to each one individually as he wills.

1 CORINTHIANS 12:4–11

Now you are the body of Christ and individually members of it. And God has appointed in the church first apostles, second prophets, third teachers, then miracles, then gifts of healing, helping, administrating, and various kinds of tongues. Are all apostles? Are all prophets? Are all teachers? Do all work miracles? Do all possess gifts of healing? Do all speak with tongues? Do all interpret? But earnestly desire the higher gifts.

1 CORINTHIANS 12:27–31

To me, though I am the very least of all the saints, this grace was given, to preach to the Gentiles the unsearchable riches of Christ, and to bring to light for everyone what is the plan of the mystery hidden for ages in God who created all things, so that through the church the manifold wisdom of God might now be made known to the rulers and authorities in the heavenly places. This was according to the eternal purpose that he has realized in Christ Jesus our Lord, in whom we have boldness and access with confidence through our faith in him.

EPHESIANS 3:8–12

We ought always to give thanks to God for you, brothers, as is right, because your faith is growing abundantly, and the love of every one of you for one another is increasing. Therefore we ourselves boast about you in the churches of God for your stead-fastness and faith in all your persecutions and in the afflictions that you are enduring.

2 THESSALONIANS 1:3–4

Is anyone among you sick? Let him call for the elders of the church, and let them pray over him, anointing him with oil in the name of the Lord.

JAMES 5:14

PRAYERS FOR CHRISTIAN WITNESS

And I heard the voice of the Lord saying, "Whom shall I send, and who will go for us?" Then I said, "Here am I! Send me."

ISAIAH 6:8

Put in the sickle,
for the harvest is ripe.
Go in, tread,
for the winepress is full.
The vats overflow,
for their evil is great.
Multitudes, multitudes,
in the valley of decision!

For the day of the LORD is near
in the valley of decision.
The sun and the moon are darkened,
and the stars withdraw their shining.
The LORD roars from Zion,
and utters his voice from Jerusalem,
and the heavens and the earth quake.
But the LORD is a refuge to his people,
a stronghold to the people of Israel.

JOEL 3:13–16

And Jesus went throughout all the cities and villages, teaching in their synagogues and proclaiming the gospel of the kingdom and healing every disease and every affliction. When he saw the crowds, he had compassion for them, because they were harassed and helpless, like sheep without a shepherd. Then he said to his disciples, "The harvest is plentiful, but the laborers are few; therefore pray earnestly to the Lord of the harvest to send out laborers into his harvest."

MATTHEW 9:35–38

And Jesus said to them, "Follow me, and I will make you become fishers of men."

MARK 1:17

And he said to them, "Go into all the world and proclaim the gospel to the whole creation."

MARK 16:15

Jesus said to them, "My food is to do the will of him who sent me and to accomplish his work. Do you not say, 'There are yet four months, then comes the harvest'? Look, I tell you, lift up your eyes, and see that the fields are white for harvest. Already the one who reaps is receiving wages and gathering fruit for eternal life, so that sower and reaper may rejoice together. For here the saying holds true, 'One sows and another reaps.' I sent you to reap that for which you did not labor. Others have labored, and you have entered into their labor."

JOHN 4:34–38

"But you will receive power when the Holy Spirit has come upon you, and you will be my witnesses in Jerusalem and in all Judea and Samaria, and to the end of the earth."

ACTS 1:8

As for you, always be sober-minded, endure suffering, do the work of an evangelist, fulfill your ministry.

2 TIMOTHY 4:5

AFTERWORD

The Grammar of Prayer: The Jesus Prayer

Like so much of Jesus' life and teaching, his response to the disciples' request for instruction on prayer took an unexpected turn (Luke 11:2–4). With his teaching on prayer, he redefined how his Jewish listeners (and his Christian followers) were to address God in prayer. Jesus took a common Jewish prayer, called a kaddish, and reformulated it in significant ways, changing the vocabulary and grammar. The kaddish would surely have been known to his disciples, though it is less familiar to readers today.

THE JEWISH KADDISH

Kaddish means "holy." The kaddish was a common prayer that all Jewish people recited on a regular basis. The Kaddish HaShem, one version of several Jewish prayers, goes like this:

> Glorified and sanctified be God's great name throughout the world He has created according to His will.

207

May He establish His kingdom in your lifetime and in
your days, and in the lifetimes of the entire House of
Israel, swiftly and soon. Now respond: Amen.

Does this prayer sound even vaguely familiar? It
should.

Jesus reintroduced the common practice of prayer. In
Jesus' day, prayer had become public-private devotion,
a piety directed both toward God and toward other
people. Dale Bruner, in his commentary *The Christbook*,
suggests that

> public-private devotion was a contradiction in terms;
> Jesus was not happy with prayer that tried to be a wit-
> ness. Prayer is not a form of evangelism, addressed to
> other people. Prayer is addressed to God. . . . There
> are subtle ways we can show others that we pray.
> Directing an activity that is supposed to be directed
> to God into an activity that can also make a good
> impression on others, Jesus calls phony.[2]

So in Matthew 6:5–6 Jesus makes the crooked kaddish straight.

> *"When you pray, you must not be like the hypocrites. For
> they love to stand and pray in the synagogues and at the
> street corners, that they may be seen by others. Truly, I
> say to you, they have received their reward. But when
> you pray, go into your room and shut the door and pray
> to your Father who is in secret. And your Father who sees
> in secret will reward you."*

Jesus is not excluding public prayer meetings, or praying out loud, but rather he is excluding showy public piety with the appearance of private devotion to God. The "room" was the supply room in the average Palestinian home. It was the only room in poor Palestinian farm houses that could be locked. It was used to store feed, small animals, tools, or other household supplies. The point was, it could be locked from the inside. It was private. But notice also that it is no longer the Holy of Holies that is the special meeting place between God and the believer; it is the "secular" space of a common supply room. "Sacred space" is replaced by "secular space." Jesus is warning against inauthentic prayer; prayer that makes public what should remain private.[3]

Jesus outlines how not to pray! In Matthew 6:7–8 our Lord explains what to avoid in prayer:

> *"When you pray, do not heap up empty phrases as the Gentiles do, for they think that they will be heard for their many words. Do not be like them, for your Father knows what you need before you ask him."*

Jesus teaches us to address God with few words as opposed to many words. Why? Repetition was the soul of pagan prayer. In fact, Seneca taught people to "fatigue the gods" with their verbosity (*Epistulae*, 31:5). The formula for pagan prayer was simple: "Much prayer = much answer." Pagan prayer rests on the belief that God is reluctant to listen to prayer; therefore his attention must be purchased, in this case by many words and much time invested in prayer. Pagans assumed they could capture God's attention by means of redundant activity instead of by relying on his mercy. Jesus teaches his disciples that since God already knows our needs before we ask him, we need not attempt to overwhelm him with repetitious requests. God is not reluctant. He's our Heavenly Father, and he cares deeply about us.

Jesus teaches a new way to pray and in so doing gives his disciples, and us, a handrail for prayer. Scot McKnight, in his book *The Jesus Creed*,[4] refers to this prayer in Matthew 6: 9–13 as "the Jesus Prayer." Notice its succinctness:

> *"Pray then like this: 'Our Father in heaven, hallowed be your name. Your kingdom come, your will be done, on earth as it is in heaven. Give us this day our daily bread, and forgive us our debts, as we also have forgiven our debtors. And lead us not into temptation, but deliver us from evil.'"*

THE JESUS PRAYER

Jesus takes a familiar prayer, the kaddish, and makes it new—the Jesus Prayer. In what ways does he begin with a simple, formulaic Jewish prayer and change the grammar to make it a model for us?

1. The Jesus Prayer begins with *Abba*—"Daddy."
2. The Jesus Prayer petitions only to sanctify the Father's name.
3. The Jesus Prayer removes the "swiftly and soon" language.

4. The Jesus Prayer adds a request that the Father's "will be done, on earth as it is in heaven."

5. The Jesus Prayer adds three "love of others" lines, dealing with bread, forgiveness, and temptation.

6. The Jesus Prayer moves from "your" to "us" in two parts: *your* petitions; *us* petitions.

7. The Jesus Prayer doesn't include an "amen."

SIX PETITIONS OF THE JESUS PRAYER

Love of Father Petitions	Love of Others Petitions
Your *name* **be hallowed.** **A petition for God to make himself central.** We don't hallow God's name. He does.	*Give us our bread, day by day.* **A petition for the present**
Your *kingdom* **come.** **A petition for God to make himself known as king.** The kingdom of God is established **by God** for us, not **by us** for God.	*Forgive us our sins as we forgive others.* **A petition for the removal of a bad past in order that we might have a good present.**
Your *will* **be done on earth as it is in heaven.** **A petition for heaven on earth.**	*Lead us not into temptation, but deliver us from evil.* **A petition for a good future.** (The Greek word for "deliver us" is a violent word for "rescue.")

Why did Jesus amend this Jewish prayer? In doing so he changed the God-only kaddish to the God-and-others Jesus Prayer.

Jesus is our Prayer Mentor. He provides us with a prayer to bring heaven to earth every day. What do we learn from Jesus, our Prayer Mentor?

211

1. We learn a new way to approach God: as our Abba.
Abba is an Aramaic word that depicts God as accessible,
strong, and tender. The term speaks to his supernatural
power and care. God is in a very real sense the Super-
Father, and Jesus is passing on to us, as God's adopted
children, his own priceless relationship with the Father.
Only now, on the basis of Christ's atoning death and resurrection, can we approach God as Father—not as "our
heavenly parent," but as "our heavenly Papa." A child's
father is the one responsible for the child. He is not only
the child's friend but also his or her parent, guardian,
and provider. In the case of our Heavenly Father, he
is also our Lord. *Father* is the signature term used by
Jesus, marking the beginning of his teaching about God.
The basis of prayer is the good Father, not the good
disciples.

Why does Jesus teach us to approach God as our
Father? To arouse within us a sense of God's uncondi-
tional, unlimited, unwavering love. The fundamental
premises of spiritual formation are that God loves us and
that we are his children. God *is* love, and love is what
he does. Since there is no perfect father on earth, we
have no perfect sense of love to transfer to our image of
God. Our heart openings are rusted shut because of the
inevitable shortfalls by which our earthly fathers loved
us—or the degree to which they failed to love us. Scot
McKnight remarks, "When we use the Jesus Prayer to
guide our prayers we rub the oil of the Jesus Creed into
the chambers of our heart."[5] The good news is that our
hearts have been especially calibrated to open to God's

love, and Jesus alone has the key. Jesus wants us to be reminded daily that our Heavenly Super-Father loves us. As you begin each new day, offer a short prayer of gratitude: "Father, thank you for loving us." The Jesus Prayer models a way of prayer that reinforces this reality on a daily basis.

2. *We learn what God wants: heaven on earth.* "Your will be done, on earth as it is in heaven." God wants his kingdom to rule on earth, just as it does in heaven. And he wants to use us to bring heaven to earth. Earth is the Father's new frontier; heaven is already fully under his sway. In this prayer we are learning about yearning. Jesus doesn't want us simply to *learn* a prayer; he wants us to *yearn* a prayer. Prayer isn't primarily about bringing our wants to God but about reporting to him for duty. What are we saying to God when we pray the Jesus Prayer? We're offering ourselves in his service to others. We're coming before our Heavenly Father, asking, "Father, how can I join you today in bringing heaven to earth?" Frank Laubach observes: "The Lord's Prayer is not a prayer to God to do something we want done. It is more nearly God's prayer to us, to help him do what he wants done."[6]

3. *We learn whom God wants us to pray for: others.* Jesus is demonstrating for us how to turn "me prayer" into "we prayer." Our Brother reminds us that none of us is an "only child"; besides himself, we have adopted siblings. This amendment stands out sharply. The Jesus Prayer isn't a God-and-me petition like the Jewish kaddish; it's a God-and-others petition. This is how we turn

the Jesus Creed (loving God and loving people) into prayer. We approach the Father with his children: our family.

4. *We learn what God believes everyone needs.* Jesus teaches us to hang our prayers on what he knows we need instead of on what we think we need.

- He knows we need bread: adequate provisions in all areas of our lives, day by day.
- He knows we need forgiveness: spiritual freedom from our sins of the past, as well as from our continuing sin nature.
- He knows we need deliverance: moral stability for the future. He asks—and teaches us to ask—that we will be spared temptation so we can accomplish the mission to which we have been called.

In the Jesus Prayer our Lord turned prayer upside down. He redefined and rearranged its terms so that we might live well as we learn how better to love God and other people.[7]

Perspectives on Prayer

I cannot answer all the curious questions of the brain concerning prayer and law, not half of them, indeed, and I will not attempt to; but I will cast my anchor here in this revealing fact, that He, the Holiest of the Holy and the Wisest of the Wise, He prays. Therefore I am assured that this anchorage of Divine example will hold the vessel in the tossings of the wildest sea of doubt, and I shall be as safe as He was, if the vessel itself is engulfed in the waves of suffering and sorrow. His act is an argument. His prayer is an inspiration. His achievements are the everlasting and all-sufficient vindication of prayer.

JOHN CLIFFORD

The Christian on his knees sees more than the philosopher on tiptoe.

DWIGHT L. MOODY

Its ground: God, by whose goodness it springeth in us.

Its use: to turn our will to His will.

Its end: to be made one with Him and like to Him in all things.

JULIANA OF NORWICH

It was no exceptional thing for Jesus to withdraw Himself "into the wilderness to pray." He was never for one moment of any day out of touch with God. He was speaking and listening to the Father all day long; and yet He, who was in such constant touch with God, felt the need as well as the joy, of more prolonged and more quiet communion with Him. . . . Most of the reasons that drive us to pray for strength and forgiveness could never have driven Him; and yet He needed prayer.

G. H. KNIGHT

The tragedy of our day is not unanswered prayer but unoffered prayer.

J. SIDLOW BAXTER

Men may spurn our appeals, reject our message, oppose our arguments, despise our person, but they are helpless against our prayers.

J. SIDLOW BAXTER

Prayer is a powerful thing, for God has bound and tied Himself to it. None can believe how powerful prayer is, and what it is able to effect, but those who have learned it by experience.

MARTIN LUTHER

Perhaps there cannot be a better way of judging of what manner of spirit we are of, than to see whether the actions of our life are such as we may safely commend them to God in our prayers.

WILLIAM LAW

Even if all the things that people prayed for happened, which they do not, this would not prove what Christians mean by the efficacy of prayer. For prayer is request. The essence of request, as distinct from compulsion, is that it may or may not be granted.

And if an infinitely wise Being listens to the requests of finite and foolish creatures, of course He will sometimes grant and sometimes refuse them. Invariable "success" in prayer would not prove the Christian doctrine at all. It would prove something more like magic—a power in certain human beings to control, or compel, the course of nature.

C. S. LEWIS

Meanwhile, little people like you and me, if our prayers are sometime granted, beyond all hope and probability, had better not draw hasty conclusions to our own advantage. If we were stronger, we might be less tenderly treated. If we were braver, we might be sent, with far less help, to defend far more desperate posts in great battle.

C. S. LEWIS

The discussion of prayer is so great that it requires the Father to reveal it, His firstborn Word to teach it, and the Spirit to enable us to think and speak rightly of so great a subject.

ORIGEN

God usually answers our prayers so much more according to the measure of His own magnificence, than of our asking, that we do not recognize His benefits to be those for which we sought Him.

COVENTRY PATMORE

The Divine Wisdom has given us prayer, not as a means whereby to obtain the good things of earth, but as a means whereby we learn to do without them; not as a means whereby we escape evil, but as a means whereby we become strong to meet it.

FREDERICK W. ROBERTSON

There is not in the world a kind of life more sweet and delightful than that of a continual conversation with God.

BROTHER LAWRENCE

Prayer is not an argument with God to persuade Him to move things our way, but an exercise by which we are enabled by His Spirit to move ourselves His way.

LEONARD RAVENHILL

The criterion for our intercessory prayer is not our earnestness, not our faithfulness, nor even our faith in God, but simply God Himself. He has taken the initiative from the beginning, and has built our prayers into the structure of the universe. He then asks us to present these requests to Him that He may show His gracious hand.

CHARLES H. TROUTMAN

Prayer Resources

Many books have been written about why and how we pray. These books do an extraordinary service of answering some of the knotty questions about prayer, and several make clear the importance of Scripture and prayer.

Ken Boa. *Handbook to Prayer: Praying Scripture Back to God*. Atlanta: Trinity House Publishers, 1993.

Dietrich Bonhoeffer. *Psalms: The Prayer Book of the Bible*. Minneapolis: Augsburg Fortress, 1970.

Walter Brueggemann. *Israel's Praise: Doxology Against Idolatry and Ideology*. Minneapolis: Augsburg Fortress, 1988.

Frederick Dale Bruner. *The Christbook: Matthew, a Commentary*. Grand Rapids, MI: Eerdmans, 2007.

Richard Foster. *Prayer: Finding the Heart's True Home*. New York: HarperOne, 1992.

Bill Hybels. *Too Busy Not to Pray: Slowing Down to Be with God*. Downers Grove, IL: InterVarsity Press, 1998.

Peter Kreeft. *Prayer: The Great Conversation*. Ft. Collins, CO: Ignatius Press, 1991.

———. *Prayer for Beginners*. Ft. Collins, CO: Ignatius Press, 2000.

C. S. Lewis. *Letters to Malcolm: Chiefly on Prayer*. New York: Harcourt, 1964.

————. *Reflections on the Psalms*. New York: Harcourt, 1958.

Scot McKnight. *The Jesus Creed: Loving God, Loving Others*. Orleans, MA: Paraclete, 2004.

Thomas Merton. *Praying the Psalms*. Collegeville, MN: Liturgical Press, 1956.

Ben Patterson. *Deepening Your Conversation with God: Learning to Love to Pray*. Minneapolis: Bethany, 2001.

————. *God's Prayer Book: The Power and Pleasure of Praying the Psalms*. Wheaton, IL: Tyndale House, 2008.

————. *NIV Prayer Devotional Bible*. Grand Rapids, MI: Zondervan, 2004.

Eugene Peterson. *Answering God: The Psalms as Tools for Prayer*. New York: HarperOne, 1991.

Richard Rohr. *Everything Belongs: The Gift of Contemplative Prayer*. New York: Crossroad, 2003.

Philip Yancey. *Prayer: Does It Make Any Difference?* Grand Rapids, MI: Zondervan, 2006.

Notes

1. Available online at http://www.spurgeongems.org/vols43-45/chs2644.pdf.

2. Dale Bruner, *The Christbook: Matthew, a Commentary* (Grand Rapids, MI: Eerdmans, 2007), 233–234.

3. Ibid., 234.

4. Scot McKnight, *The Jesus Creed: Loving God, Loving Others* (Orleans, MA: Paraclete, 2004), 14.

5. Ibid.

6. Frank C. Laubach, *Prayer, the Mightiest Force in the World* (Whitefish, MT: Kessinger Publishing, 2007), 40.

7. Adapted from unpublished material by Tim Cosby, Pastor of Discipleship, Bella Vista Church, Grand Rapids, Michigan. Used by permission.